TRAVELLERS

LONDON

By
KATHY ARNOLD

Written by Kathy Arnold, updated by Claire Boobbyer
Original photography by Robert Mort, updated photography by Neil Setchfield

Published by Thomas Cook Publishing
A division of Thomas Cook Tour Operations Limited
Company registration no. 3772199 England
The Thomas Cook Business Park, 9 Coningsby Road,
Peterborough PE3 8SB, United Kingdom
Email: books@thomascook.com, Tel: +44 (0) 1733 416477
www.thomascookpublishing.com

Produced by Cambridge Publishing Management Limited
Burr Elm Court, Main Street, Caldecote CB23 7NU

ISBN: 978-1-84848-146-6

© 2007 Thomas Cook Publishing
This second edition © 2009
Text © Thomas Cook Publishing
Maps © Thomas Cook Publishing
Reproduced by permission of Ordnance Survey on behalf of HMSO.
© Crown Copyright 2009. All rights reserved. Ordnance Survey Licence number 100035725.
Transport map © Transport for London

Series Editor: Maisie Fitzpatrick
Production/DTP: Steven Collins

Printed and bound in Italy by Printer Trento S.r.l.

Cover photography: Front L–R: © Shangara Singh/Alamy; © Pictures Colour Library/Alamy; © Nigel Watkins/Alamy
Back: © Paul Panavlotou/4CR

All rights reserved. No part of this publication may be reproduced, stored in a retrieval system or transmitted, in any form or by any means, electronic, mechanical, recording or otherwise, in any part of the world, without prior permission of the publisher. Requests for permission should be made to the publisher at the above address.

Although every care has been taken in compiling this publication, and the contents are believed to be correct at the time of printing, Thomas Cook Tour Operations Limited cannot accept any responsibility for errors or omissions, however caused, or for changes in details given in the guidebook, or for the consequences of any reliance on the information provided. Descriptions and assessments are based on the author's views and experiences when writing and do not necessarily represent those of Thomas Cook Tour Operations Limited.

Contents

Background	4–15
Introduction	4
Land and people	6
History	8
Politics	10
Culture	12
Calendar of events	14

First steps	16–21
Impressions	16

Destination guide	22–117
London, old and new	22
British Museum	24
Buckingham Palace	26
The royal connection	28
London churches	40
The City	42
Covent Garden	50
Dickens' London	52
Docklands	54
Lesser-known London	62
Monuments, statues and sculptures	72
Museum of London	74
Museum in Docklands	76
National Gallery	78
St Paul's Cathedral	86
The Science Museum	88
The South Bank Centre	92
Tate Galleries	94
The Tower of London	100
All around the Tower	102
Victoria and Albert Museum	106
Westminster Abbey	110
Westminster and Parliament	112
Whitehall and Trafalgar Square	114

KEY TO MAPS
- ⊖ Underground (Tube) station
- ★ Start of walk/drive
- ●— DLR station

Getting away from it all	118–37
Day trips from London	132

Directory	138–89
Shopping	138
Entertainment	146
Children	152
Sport and leisure	158
Food and drink	164
Hotels and accommodation	176
Practical guide	180

Index	190–91

Features
Churches	38
The City	44
Ethnic London	56
London's lungs	116
Shopper's Eden	144
Afternoon tea	170
London pubs	172

Maps
Central London	18–19
London environs	20–21
Royal London walk	31
Chelsea walk	35
Chiswick and Hammersmith walk	37
Financial London walk	47
Saints and sinners walk	49
Docklands	54–5
Legal London walk	69
Gentlemen's London walk	84
Theatreland and Bohemian London walk	98
Bards and bawds walk	105
Victoria and Albert walk	109
The Thames: Charing Cross to Woolwich	125
The Thames: Charing Cross to Hampton Court	126–7
London Underground	188–9

Introduction

'When a man is tired of London he is tired of life.'

SAMUEL JOHNSON *(1709–84)*

London today is one of the greatest cities in the world, as it was one hundred years ago, capital of the world's first industrialised nation and hub of the British Empire, the largest the world has ever seen. Although Britain is no longer the predominant world power, London retains its prominent position, recognised as a centre of arts such as theatre and music, and finance.

The 'City of London', a commercial centre since Roman times, is one of the world's three major financial powerhouses. Landmarks like Big Ben, Tower Bridge and Buckingham Palace are familiar to millions. It is a city rich in history which everyone wants to see at least once in a lifetime, though one visit barely skims the surface of its 2,000-year story.

Capital of the UK ...
Over 7 million people live in Greater London, capital of the United Kingdom (England, Wales, Scotland and Northern Ireland) which has a population of 60 million.

The country is governed and administered from London. Parliament meets here to make laws, and the constitutional monarch, Queen Elizabeth II, also lives here.

. . . City of the world
One of London's, and indeed Britain's, greatest exports, the English language,

THOMAS COOK'S LONDON

Thomas Cook's first organised trip to London was a landmark in his travel business. He arranged a tour to the 1851 Great Exhibition in Hyde Park. This was the first trip on which he had to plan accommodation for his working-class clientele. He found dormitory dwellings for all of them at £2 per day, including breakfast, with a penny extra for cleaning their boots.

Over 165,000 people took Cook's trip to the Exhibition that season. The trip, however, was nearly put out of business by undercutting of prices by the Northern Railway (Cook's trip ran with the Midland Railway). Discount wars are nothing new!

is now the international language of the world. Yet, Londoners can hear some 300 languages being spoken around them. In fact, more than a third of its population comprises various ethnic minority groups. This diverse mixture of cultures is reflected in music and markets, religions and restaurants. No wonder each of the capital's annual 26 million visitors can find a link with home.

'London is a mart for many nations who resort to it by land and sea.'
VENERABLE BEDE, (8th century)

'London doesn't love the latent or the lurking … It wants cash over the counter and letters ten feet high.'
HENRY JAMES, *The Awkward Age*, 1899

'… in sleepy London town there's just no place for a street fighting man!'
MICK JAGGER and **KEITH RICHARDS**, *Street Fighting Man*, 1968 song

'London is a riddle. Paris is an explanation.'
GK CHESTERTON, 1908

'I don't know what London's coming to – the higher the buildings, the lower the morals.'
NOËL COWARD, 1899–1973 *Collected Sketches and Lyrics*

'In the city time becomes visible.'
LEWIS MUMFORD, 1961

'More than any other city in Europe London is a show, living by bluff.'
JAN MORRIS, 1980

'When it's three o'clock in New York, it's still 1938 in London.'
BETTE MIDLER, 1978, quoted in *The Times*

'London Pride has been handed down to us.'
NOËL COWARD, 1941

'The English … are already hard to find in London. No one lives there who is not paid to do so.'
EVELYN WAUGH, 1959

'At any given point London looks huge.'
HENRY JAMES, *Portraits of Places*, 1883

The griffin, symbol of the City of London

Land and people

Geologically, the earth on which London is built is young. The oldest rock in the UK is 2,600 million years old. The mix of sand and clay that lies under much of London is less than 70 million years old – laid down by receding waters. The chalk and flint under south London is between 70 and 135 million years old.

The shape of the land

London lies in the flat southeast of England, which by 6000 BC had become separated by water from the continent of Europe.

It is an estuary capital, built near the mouth of the River Thames which bisects the city. Within Greater London, high open areas at Hampstead, Blackheath and Richmond offer distant views of the whole city.

Over the centuries England has been gradually tilting, causing a slight sinking in the east. The Thames is tidal right through London, so when the waters are swollen by surge tides from the North Sea, flooding is a danger. The Thames Barrier at Woolwich was built to prevent such a disaster.

Climate

Prevailing winds blow from the southwest, making the climate temperate and damp. London's weather is changeable, frequently reflected in the weather forecast of 'cloudy with sunny intervals'.

Extremes of temperature are rare, and the pea-soup fogs once caused by coal fires and made famous in films have not been seen for half a century.

London's millions

It is thought that people first lived in the London/Thames area around 250,000 years ago.

Recorded history begins with the Romans. Londinium became the fifth largest city in the Empire with a population of perhaps 50,000 souls by AD 200.

By 1500, the medieval city still contained only 75,000 people, but underwent rapid growth during the Tudor period, reaching 200,000 by Queen Elizabeth I's death in 1603. Unbelievably, congestion then was worse than it is now. In 1801, at the first census, Georgian London boasted 959,000 citizens, and was the largest city in Europe.

As people left the land for the cities during the Industrial Revolution of the 19th century, further phenomenal growth took place. Over 5 million more people squashed into Dickensian London, so that by 1901, the metropolis numbered 6.5 million.

The boom continued, and by the start of World War II, the population had peaked at 8.6 million people. After the war, 'dormitory' towns were deliberately developed outside the city to relieve the overcrowded housing conditions. Today, while it is still one of the world's largest built-up areas, only 7 million people remain, augmented by 26 million tourists each year, of which 14 million travel from overseas.

London's population has always been cosmopolitan. After World War II the city absorbed European refugees. From the Commonwealth it welcomed West Indian immigrants in the '50s and '60s, and Indians, Pakistanis and other Asians in later decades.

Communities are on the whole mixed. Although there is an element of racial tension, new Londoners, in general, have become part of the British way of life, and have adopted some of the native characteristics.

Office workers taking a break in Soho Square

History

AD 43–410	Roman occupation. Emperor Claudius invades Britain and builds London's first bridge. Londinium established as walled city.
886	Saxon King Alfred defeats invading Danes and establishes London as an international trading centre.
1066	Last invasion of the British Isles. William of Normandy (the 'Conqueror') defeats Harold at Hastings, is crowned King at Westminster Abbey, and commissions the Tower of London.
1191	King Richard I, the Lionheart, recognises the City of London as self-governing. Henry Fitz Elywin becomes its first elected mayor.
1215	Magna Carta, the Charter of English Liberties, signed by King John.
1348–50	The Black Death – bubonic plague – decimates population of about 50,000.
1500–1600	Population of London jumps from around 75,000 to 200,000.
1605	Gunpowder plot to assassinate James I at Westminster Palace.
1642–60	Civil War. The City of London backs Parliament against the king. King Charles I beheaded, then monarchy restored as Charles II takes the throne.
1665–6	Plague kills over 100,000, and the Great Fire destroys four-fifths of the city.
1700s	Population around 575,000 – the largest city in Western Europe. The Georgian period establishes itself as a time of opulent architecture. Population begins moving to suburbs such as Hampstead and West End.
1750	Second bridge built, at Westminster.
1801	First London census: population of 959,000.

	London is also the world's largest port.		of Asian and Afro-Caribbean citizens arrive.
1811–94	Thirteen bridges across the Thames built or rebuilt in this period as London expands.	1951	Festival of Britain.
		1952	Accession of Queen Elizabeth II. Coronation in 1953.
1826–60	Buckingham Palace and current Houses of Parliament built.	1956	Clean Air Act clears the city of smog.
1837–1901	Queen Victoria's coronation (at 18). By 1851 population has reached 2,363,000. The Great Exhibition attracts 6 million visitors.	1960s	'Swinging' London: the Beatles, Carnaby Street and the King's Road all hit the headlines.
		1966	England wins World Cup football championship.
1863	Metropolitan Railway inaugurates first urban underground railway and first 'Tube' runs on the Northern line (1890).	1973	Britain joins European Community.
		1981–95	The opening of London City Airport and Docklands Light Railway, Canary Wharf.
1897	Victoria's silver jubilee.
1915	World War I. London attacked by German zeppelins.
		2000	Millennium celebrated with the opening of the Dome and London Eye.
1939–45	World War II. Severe bomb and fire damage. Population peaks at 8.6 million.
		2007	Opening of St Pancras Eurostar terminus.
1950s–60s	Empire evolves into 'Commonwealth' and substantial numbers	2012	London to host 2012 Olympics.

History

Politics

The United Kingdom has a monarch as its figurehead, but power lies with the government of the day, usually formed from the party with an overall majority in the elected House of Commons, currently the Labour Party. Led by the prime minister, currently Gordon Brown and his 'Cabinet' of key ministers, the government decides policy, administers the country within the framework of existing laws and places new legislation before Parliament for approval or rejection.

Parliament, sitting in the Palace of Westminster beside the Thames, consists of a House of Commons with 646 elected Members (MPs) and the nominated House of Lords (currently 746 members in total) which acts as a revising chamber for draft laws passed by the Commons. The British Parliament, the 'Mother of Parliaments', has served as a model for democratic government around the world.

London itself is administered by the Greater London Authority, which has an elected Mayor and a 25-member Assembly, whose responsibilities include development, policing and transport.

Concentration of head offices

The large Civil Service ministries, as well as the head offices of Britain's largest manufacturing and service industry companies, tend to congregate in London.

Britain was once the 'workshop of the world', but the last few decades have been a story of manufacturing decline, accompanied by a growth in service industries such as financial services, marketing, advertising and tourism.

From an export earnings point of view, the City of London is the jewel in London's crown. Thanks to its geographical position, it is possible to trade with Tokyo in the morning and Wall Street in the afternoon.

One of the world's oldest legal systems

The British system of justice is famous throughout the world. The laws can basically be divided into three parts. The oldest part of the law, originally unwritten, is common law, based on the principle of judicial precedent (past judgements used to decide current cases). The rules of equity developed to decide cases that could not be dealt with satisfactorily in common law. Statute law is formed by Acts of Parliament.

Unlike other, newer democracies, there is no written Bill of Rights, nor a written Constitution.

The concept of 'trial by jury' is at the heart of British criminal law. Courts operate with a presiding judge who advises a jury of 12 ordinary citizens. The accused is presumed innocent until proven guilty. Barristers speak for the prosecution and for the defence. The jury decides guilt or innocence; the judge decides the sentence.

Ease and unease

The British capital is in the affluent southeast of England which has 30 per cent of the population and 36 per cent of the economic output. London itself contains a broad spectrum of people, from some of the world's richest to the homeless, living on the streets.

In recent years incomes per head in Greater London have been well above the national average, and twice what workers in some rural areas receive. The high price of land in the capital, however, means private housing is expensive, so many workers have moved to dormitory towns outside the city.

Although there has been an increase in crimes against property, particularly cars, London is still regarded as a reasonably safe city.

The new Europe

As an island, Britain has enjoyed relative peace compared with continental Europe. Politically and financially, however, Britain's future – and therefore London's – lies in ever closer links with its EU partners.

The Gothic Victorian splendour of the Royal Courts of Justice

Culture

London is a city of contradictions. It is a metropolis of some 1,580sq km (610sq miles), yet it is made up of recognisable areas, even villages, each with its own identity, history and legends. Full of pageantry and culture to suit all tastes, London welcomes its visitors, and is all things to all men, women and children.

Living theatre

The London stage is alive and well with 600 productions a year, ranging from Shakespeare to Andrew Lloyd Webber and outstanding productions from countries around the world. You can see opera, drama, comedy, and musicals – the best of which often take the world by storm.

The visual arts

Visit the commercial galleries between Piccadilly and Oxford Street to enjoy some of the best of contemporary painting and sculpture. Go to the Royal Academy Summer Exhibition to appreciate the works of living British artists. Meanwhile, the National Gallery, the Tate Britain and Tate Modern galleries, the Victoria and Albert Museum and the British Museum offer a greater collection of paintings and treasures to admire and enjoy than any other city on earth.

Public sculpture in London tends to be straightforward commemorative statuary, but look for off-beat works in unexpected places: a Barbara Hepworth on the exterior of the John Lewis department store in Oxford Street, for example, or a Henry Moore on the Mall in the shadow of Admiralty Arch.

Music, opera and ballet

No less than five major orchestras flourish in London, including the London Symphony Orchestra and the Royal Philharmonic. They give world-class performances of the classical repertoire under some of the best conductors in the world at famous venues such as the Royal Festival Hall and the Royal Albert Hall. The Royal Opera House, with its own opera and ballet company, rivals any other such institution anywhere in the world.

Major rock and pop concerts go on non-stop in London, and minority interests such as live jazz, folk and country music are catered for, too.

Living architecture

The Palace of Westminster, Whitehall, Westminster Abbey, Trafalgar Square, the National Gallery, St Paul's, Buckingham Palace ... London has some of the grandest architecture in the world. The city is, however, not an architectural museum, and in the new and developing Docklands east of the city, the modern landmark Canary Wharf Tower is, for the moment, the country's tallest building.

Living language

London is the home of the world's most widespread language, but there is still local slang. A 'cuppa' is a cup of tea, the Londoner's favourite non-alcoholic drink. A 'pint' in a pub means a pint (56.8cl) of beer. The underground railway is the 'Tube'. Taxis are often 'cabs', from the French *cabriolet*, and still have 'hackney' licences, derived from the French *haquenée*, meaning 'ambling nag'.

Cockney rhyming slang survives and can still be heard in certain areas of London, notably the East End, and in the markets. Originally a code among street folk, the colourful phrases can still be heard. 'Apples and pears' rhymes with stairs, 'tit for tat' with hat; in the code, only the first part of the catchphrase is used, so stairs are 'apples', and a hat is a 'titfer'.

The greatest shows on Earth

London presents military pageantry and great sporting events supremely well. There's Trooping the Colour, a military parade where the Queen takes the salute on her official birthday; the Lord Mayor's Show, a colourful procession through the City of London; the Football Association (FA) Cup Final at Wembley Stadium, recently rebuilt with seating capacity for 90,000 spectators; the Oxford and Cambridge Boat Race; the Royal Ascot and Derby horse races; and the Wimbledon Lawn Tennis Championships. Since 1981, the London Marathon has been an added fixture.

Cultural history encapsulated: Shakespeare's Globe Theatre

Calendar of events

ROYAL AND SOCIAL CALENDAR

Expect members of the Royal Family at many of these annual events which often date back centuries. **Royal Salutes:** *a 41-gun salute is fired in Hyde Park at noon, and a 62-gun salute at the Tower of London at 1pm (62 for the Sovereign, 41 for others).*

January			
6th	Epiphany Service	Gold, frankincense and myrrh offered on Sovereign's behalf	Chapel Royal, St James
February			
6th	Accession Day	Queen Elizabeth II, 1952	Royal Gun Salutes
March			
	Royal Film Performance	Charity gala	West End Cinema
April			
21st	Queen's Birthday	Queen Elizabeth II, born 1926	Royal Gun Salutes
May			
Late	Chelsea Flower Show	One of world's finest	Royal Hospital, Chelsea
June			
2nd	Coronation Day	Queen Elizabeth II, 1953	Royal Gun Salutes
1st Wednesday and Thursday	Beating Retreat Parade	Ceremonial Marching Bands	Horse Guards Parade
1st Saturday	Derby Day	Famous horse race	Epsom Downs Racecourse
2nd Saturday	Queen's Official Birthday	Trooping the Colour and Royal Gun Salutes	Horse Guards Parade
Mid-month (Mon)	Garter Ceremony	Knights of the Garter	Windsor Castle
Mid-month (Tue–Fri)	Royal Ascot	Horse race meeting, famous for ladies' headwear	Ascot Racecourse
10th	Prince Philip's Birthday	Born 1921	Royal Gun Salutes
Late June/July	Wimbledon	World's No 1 Tennis Tournament	Wimbledon
July			
Mid-month	Royal Tournament	Indoor military manoeuvres	Earl's Court
	Royal Garden Parties	Tea for 8,000	Buckingham Palace
	Investitures	Distributing honours	Buckingham Palace
November			
Usually mid-month	State Opening of Parliament	Procession to Palace of Westminster	From Buckingham Palace
2nd Saturday	Festival of Remembrance	For the war dead	Royal Albert Hall
2nd Sunday	Remembrance Service	For the war dead	Cenotaph, Whitehall
Late	Royal Command Performance	Charity Gala	West End Theatre
December			
	Investitures	Distributing honours	Buckingham Palace

EVENTS

No 'Royals', but always very busy.

January
Early	Sales	Bargains galore in shops	Everywhere
Early	London Boat Show	For seadogs and landlubbers	ExCel, Docklands

February
	Chinese New Year	Dragon dancers, fire crackers (weekend)	Soho

March
Mid-month	Chelsea Antiques Fair	Authentic antiques	Chelsea Old Town Hall
Easter Good Friday	Distribution of Hot Cross Buns	Butterworth Charity	St Bartholomew the Great
Easter Sunday	Easter Parade	Easter bonnets and all	Battersea Park
Easter Monday	Harness Horse Parade	Old-fashioned splendour	Battersea Park

April
1st	April Fools' Day	Check press – carefully!	
(Saturday)	Boat Race	Oxford and Cambridge Universities row from Putney to Mortlake	River Thames
	Spring Flower Show	British favourite	Royal Horticultural Society, Westminster
(Sunday)	London Marathon	The world's biggest	Blackheath to The Mall

May
1st	May Day	Union Parades	Hyde Park
2nd Sunday	Punch and Judy Festival		Covent Garden
29th	Oak Apple Day	Chelsea Pensioners Parade	Royal Hospital Chelsea

June
	Open Air Theatre	Season opens	Regent's Park

July
(2 months)	Promenade Concerts	Classical music	Royal Albert Hall
	Sales	Bargains galore in shops	Everywhere

August
On or near 1st	Doggett's Coat & Badge	Sculling Race on Thames	London Bridge to Chelsea Bridge
	Summer Flower Show	London in bloom	Royal Horticultural Society, Westminster
Bank Holiday Weekend	Notting Hill Carnival	Europe's biggest	Ladbroke Grove, Notting Hill

September
	Horseman's Sunday	Service, procession and horse show	Hyde Park

October
1st Sunday	Pearly Harvest Festival service	With Pearly Kings and Queens	St Martin-in-the-Fields, Trafalgar Square

November
5th	Bonfire Night	Guy Fawkes	Everywhere
1st Sunday	Veteran Car Run	From Hyde Park Corner	London to Brighton
2nd Saturday	Lord Mayor's Show	Parade	City of London
Mid-November	Christmas lights	Festive lights decorate	Regent Street, Oxford Street, Bond Street and Jermyn Street

December
	Christmas Celebrations	Christmas tree	Trafalgar Square

Calendar of events

Impressions

Londoners are used to seeing tourists every day of the year. The dilemma for visitors is how to meet the locals. Come to London on a package tour, stay in a big hotel, go on guided tours, stick to the major attractions, and the chances are you will never meet a Londoner. To do that, stay in a bed and breakfast, walk the city and explore the side streets. Leave the West End and go shopping in Richmond or Hampstead, drink at pubs overlooking the river or Hampstead Heath. It's not hard to end up chatting.

Meet the people

Britain, and especially London, has changed dramatically in the past 30 years. Although the 'Establishment' of old money, private schools and the aristocracy still have influence, the class system is no longer so rigid.

Beyond the Swinging Sixties

As the capital of the 'Swinging Sixties', and with personalities such as the Beatles, photographer David Bailey and fashion designer Mary Quant becoming household names around the world, London became a must-see destination from the 1960s onwards.

The older generation still talks about the stoic and cheerful 'spirit of the Blitz', which endured World War II bombing raids. That attitude resurfaces in adversity – whether it is snow, train strikes or Tube delays. Compared with dwellers in other major cities, Londoners come across as helpful, polite and tolerant. As a general rule, they don't push in crowds or on the Tube; they queue quietly, and do not blow their horns in traffic jams or shout abuse. If you follow the established unwritten rules, you will enjoy your stay.

It's quicker by Tube

London couldn't function without its 130-year-old underground or 'Tube' system that transports over 3 million passengers every day. Londoners may moan as they struggle to and from work during the rush hours, but buy a Travelcard after 9.30am (any time on weekends) and enjoy virtually unlimited travel on buses, as well as Tubes and trains. There is a comprehensive network with over-ground trains carrying commuters from London's outer suburbs, and southeast England.

How to beat the crowds

London's famous attractions are popular; all are on some tour or other, so it's worth avoiding visits in the late morning and early afternoon. Arrive at, say, the British Museum as soon as it opens, to get ahead of the rush. Drop into the National Gallery at the end of the day, perhaps on the way to a nearby theatre. As museums and galleries like these are free, you can afford to pop in more than once. Eat a little earlier or later to avoid the lunchtime crush between 1pm and 2pm.

Think local

Ignore the pressure to dash off to the Tower of London as soon as you've seen the Changing of the Guard at Buckingham Palace, wasting an hour or more on travel. Within five minutes' walk of the Palace are the Queen's Gallery, the Royal Mews, the Guards Museum and the Cabinet War Rooms. Close to the Tower are old churches, Tower Bridge, HMS *Belfast*, the Design Museum and Hay's Galleria. Save time; see more.

Save your legs

Although London is best explored on foot, two good ways to sightsee sitting down are by boat and bus. As London grew along the banks of the Thames, there is no better way to appreciate the history than by travelling as kings and queens once did, by boat, from Westminster to Greenwich. Enjoy a different view of St Paul's, the Tower and Docklands.

Alternatively, see everyday London from the top of a red bus. London Transport buses will take you all over the capital. A popular service with tourists, the Number 11 bus runs from Liverpool Street Station to Fulham Broadway past a dozen major sights, including the Bank of England, St Paul's Cathedral, the Law Courts, the Savoy Hotel, Trafalgar Square, Downing Street, the Houses of Parliament and Westminster Abbey. All for the price of an ordinary ticket or a one-day Travelcard (*see* Public Transport, *p184*).

Cost of living

Central London in particular is about 30 per cent more expensive than outer London and the rest of the country. Tourists can expect to pay inflated rates for accommodation, local travel, and eating and drinking out.

London buses are easy to use

Impressions

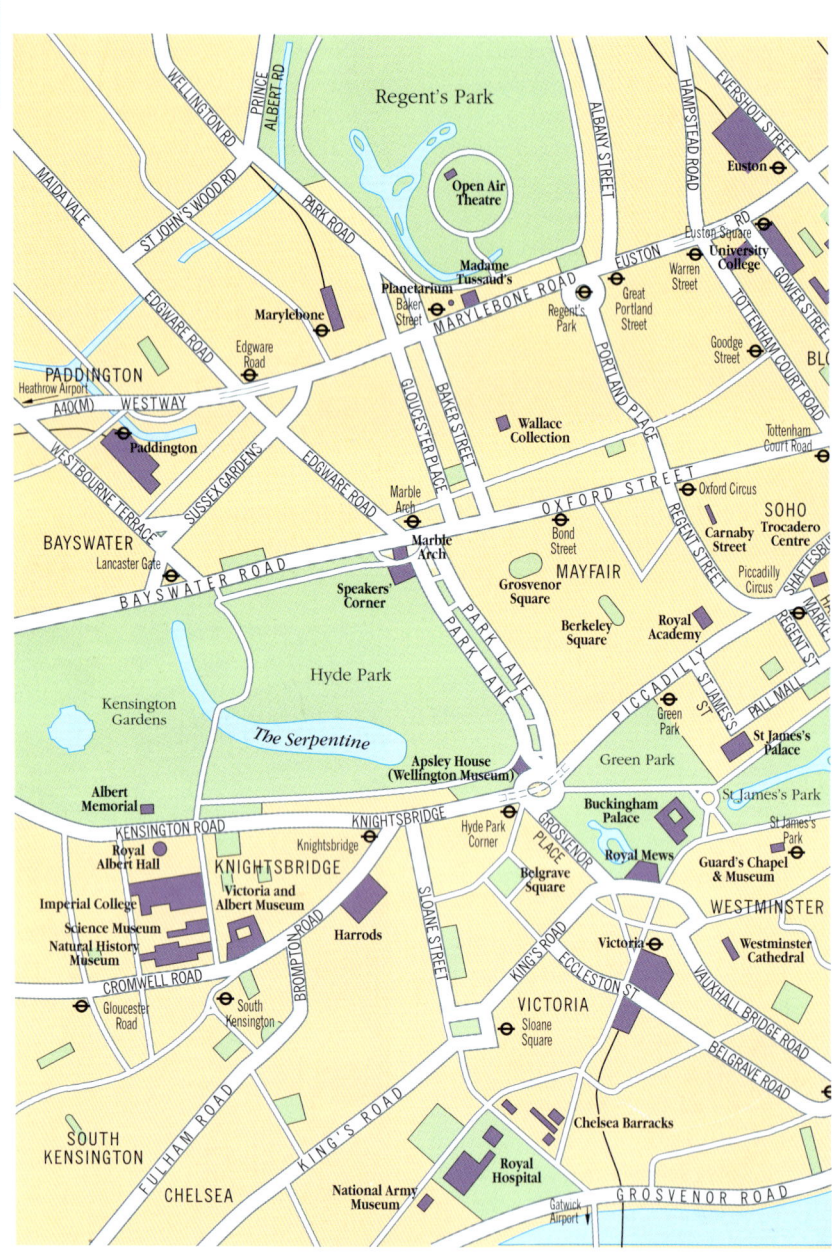

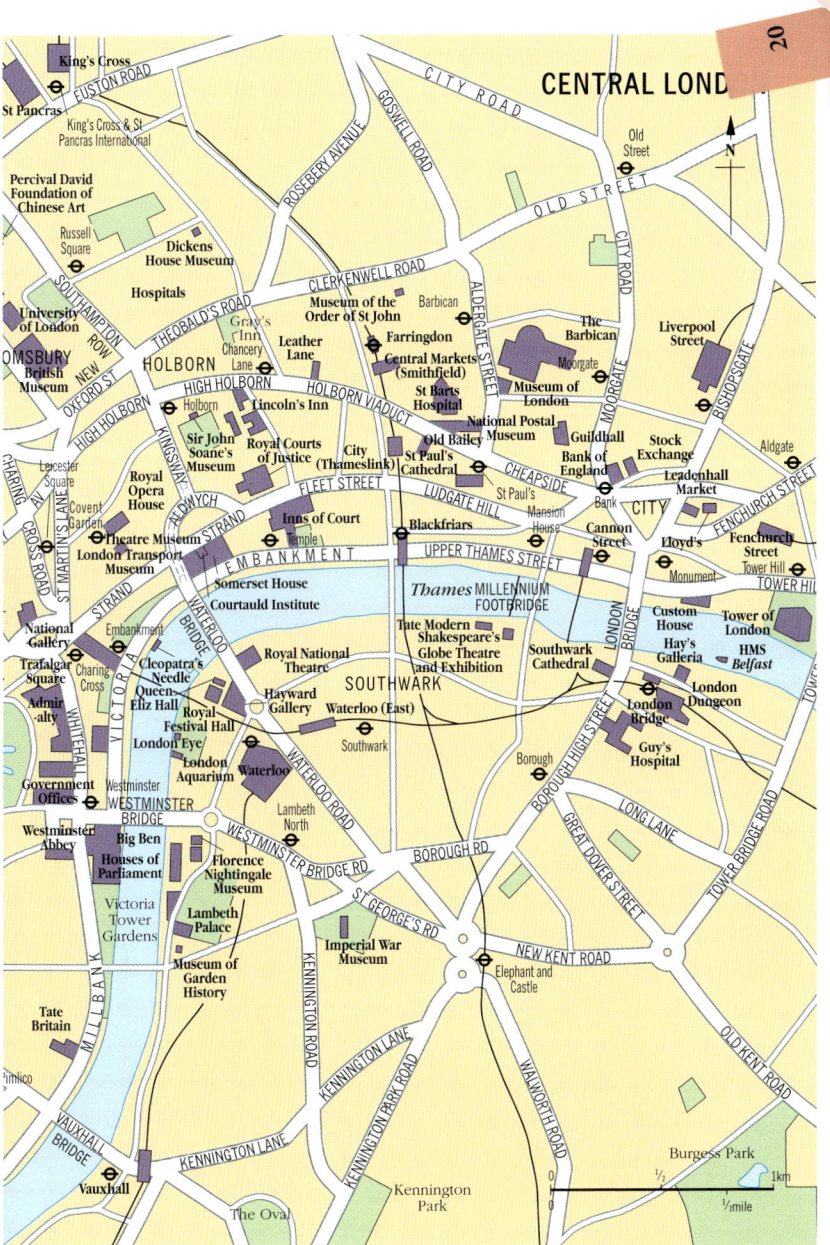

Local London

Every city has areas that are familiar to locals but not to visitors, but certain areas of London have reputations known to all. London's West End is in the geographical middle, but is so named because it is west of the original centre of the City. It's the principal entertainment and shopping area, including Leicester Square, Regent Street, Oxford Street and Bond Street.

The City is the financial area around the Bank of England and the

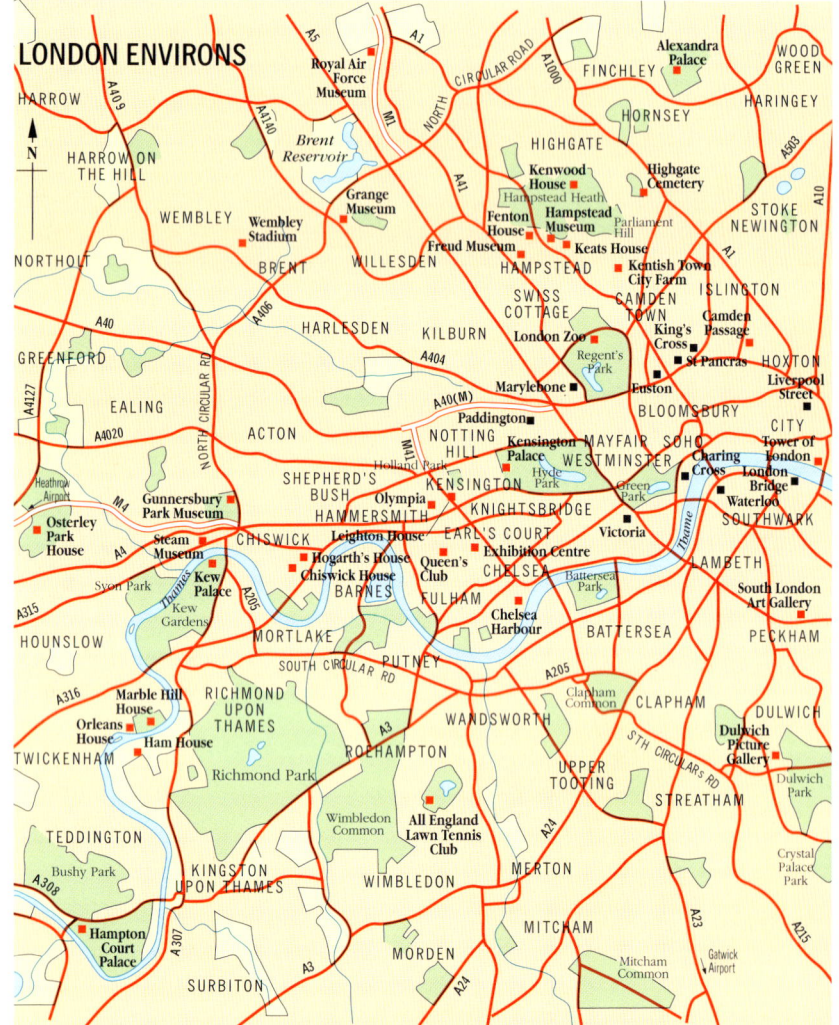

Stock Exchange. Docklands is even further east. This up-and-coming development borders one of London's least well-off areas, the East End. West London starts west of Earl's Court while North London lies north of Camden Town.

Bloomsbury: the British Museum and University of London.

Chelsea: frequented by rich, artistic and fashion-conscious people.

Covent Garden: a pot-pourri of shops, restaurants and street theatre (*see p50*).

Hampstead: for the well-off and the intellectual. Hampstead Heath is good for windy walks and views over London.

Hoxton: popular among the young set, this area was made trendy by a rising wave of British artists in the early '90s.

Kensington: includes the Kensington palaces, the V & A and Natural History museums, and the Royal Albert Hall.

Knightsbridge: home of London's smartest shops such as Harrods.

Mayfair: posh, central residential area between Hyde Park and Regent Street.

Notting Hill: hip neighbourhood in West London famous for its weekend market and annual carnival.

Soho: still London's red-light district, but also theatreland; full of trendy and interesting restaurants and bars.

Westminster: Britain's centre of government, with the Houses of Parliament, 10 Downing Street and Westminster Abbey.

London, old and new

'I got into the heart of City life. I saw and felt London at last . . . I have seen the West End, the parks, the fine squares; but I love the City far better . . .'

CHARLOTTE BRONTË, *Villette, 1853*

Albert Memorial
Built in 1876, the Prince Albert Memorial sits opposite the Royal Albert Hall. The encouragement Queen Victoria's German husband gave the arts and sciences is reflected in the frieze of 169 full-size statues of poets and musicians, painters, architects and scientists.
Kensington Gore, SW7.
Tube: South Kensington.

Apsley House
Known as 'No 1 London' because it was the first house past the toll gate, this 18th-century mansion belonged to the 'Iron Duke', the first Duke of Wellington, who made it his home after a brilliant military career which culminated in his victory over Napoleon at Waterloo in 1815. Its magnificent collection of some 4,000 works of art remains intact, and it is still lived in by the family.

The Grand Staircase was recast, and the floor reinforced to accommodate the 3.4m- (11ft-) high marble nude statue of Napoleon. Upstairs Wellington himself added the 27m- (88ft-) long Waterloo Gallery. Note the faint tri-cornered hat on Goya's *Wellington on Horseback*. X-rays have revealed that this was originally a portrait of Napoleon's brother, painted over with the likeness of Wellington after his victory at Waterloo!
149 Piccadilly, Hyde Park Corner, W1. Tel: (020) 7499 5676. www.english-heritage.org.uk/apsleyhouse. Open: Apr–Oct Wed–Sun & Bank Holidays 11am–5pm; Nov–Mar Wed–Sun 11am–4pm. Closed: 24–26 Dec, 1 Jan. Admission charge.
Tube: Hyde Park Corner

Bank of England Museum
Visitors are not allowed inside the bank itself, but its history is explained in a museum in the same building. Gold bars and banknotes, ledgers and antique iron chests are part of a display that begins with a reproduction of a 200-year-old

bank stock office with its counter and account books, and comes right up to date with a computerised dealing desk, interactive video systems and foreign exchange dealing games. Founded in 1694, the bank was the brainchild of Scottish merchant William Patterson and operated as a commercial institution, with the government as a client. Tradition remains in the pink and scarlet uniforms of the gatekeepers at the entrance. The Old Lady of Threadneedle Street, the bank's nickname, was coined in a speech in the House of Commons by Sheridan in 1797, who referred to 'an elderly lady in the City of great credit and long standing'.
Threadneedle St, museum entrance on Bartholomew Lane, EC2.
Tel: (020) 7601 5545.
www.bankofengland.co.uk/museum.
Open: Mon–Fri 10am–5pm. Closed: Public and Bank Holidays. Free admission. Tube: Bank.

The London Eye in front of County Hall (now a hotel and site of the London Aquarium)

Banqueting House, Whitehall
See Whitehall and Trafalgar Square, pp114–15.

Barbican Centre
Six thousand people live in 21 concrete towers on 24 hectares (59 acres) named after the barbican, or watchtower gate, to the ancient City of London. The redeeming feature of this bleak development is the thriving arts centre, the London home of the London Symphony Orchestra.
Silk Street, EC2. Tel: (020) 7638 4141.
www.barbican.org.uk
Tube: Moorgate or Barbican.

HMS *Belfast*
See p103.

Big Ben
See p112.

London Eye
Europe's largest observation wheel, the London Eye, offers breathtaking views of London. A giant on the city's skyline, the London Eye is a towering 135m (443ft) high. Its 32 capsules transport up to 25 passengers each, in one 30-minute revolution. The Eye is a must for every visitor to the city, as from its capsules you can see some of London's most celebrated landmarks.
Southbank, SE1. Tel: 0870 5000 600.
www.londoneye.com. Open: May–June, Sept daily 10am–9pm; July–Aug daily 10am–9.30pm; Oct–Apr, daily 10am–8pm. Admission charge. Tube: Waterloo.

British Museum

Every year up to five million visitors pay homage to one of the world's best-known museums. Inside are relics and works of art from around the world, ranging from ancient civilisations to modern times. The imposing façade, with 44 columns, is 113m (370ft) long.

Just inside the main doors is a statue of Sir Hans Sloane. This remarkable physician, naturalist, traveller and insatiable collector died in 1753, leaving his hoard of 80,000 objects to the nation. The museum was the first of its kind in the world.

A lifetime could be spent in the galleries; for those with only a few hours, however, the highlights are detailed here. There are also rooms full of Islamic and Japanese treasures. Pick up a map and 'do it yourself', or take a 90-minute guided tour. Information sheets are available for children.

GROUND FLOOR
The Rosetta Stone

The Egyptian Gallery (room 4) has impressive statues and tomb paintings, but the centre of attention is a flat, black piece of basalt covered with inscriptions: the Rosetta Stone. Discovered near Alexandria in 1799, its bilingual text is a priest's decree from 196 BC. Translated from (previously undecipherable) hieroglyphs into Greek, it unlocks the language of ancient Egypt.

The Elgin Marbles

The most famous and contentious of all the museum's treasures, the marbles, dating from the 5th century BC, were rescued by Lord Elgin in 1801, when the Turks occupying Athens were using the Parthenon for target practice. However, there is now a campaign in Greece to retrieve them.

The Great Court

Now that the British Library has moved to St Pancras, the Reading Room area has been transformed. Reputedly the largest covered public square in Europe at 0.8ha (2 acres), it is protected by a spectacular glass roof. With the Reading Room still at its heart, it has two magnificent staircases and also a restaurant.

Great Russell Street, WC1. Tel: (020) 7323 8299. www.britishmuseum.org.

Open: daily 10am–5pm. The Great Court is open Sun–Wed 9am–6pm, Thur–Sat 9am–11pm. Free admission; charge for special exhibitions. Closed: 24–26 Dec, 1 Jan & Good Friday. Special guided tours daily (charge). Free lectures. Tube: Holborn, Russell Square or Tottenham Court Rd.

UPPER FLOOR
Roman mosaic pavement

Rich relics of Britain's past continue to be discovered. At the top of the main stairs is the 50sq m (540sq ft) Roman mosaic dating back 1,600 years, found in 1963.

Lindow Man

In 1984, the preserved body of an Iron Age man (300 BC–AD 100) was found in a peat bog in the northwest of England (room 50).

Sutton Hoo treasure

Room 41 houses the richest treasure hoard ever found in Britain. Dug up in 1939, the Sutton Hoo Burial Ship had fine gold and silver jewellery from all over Europe in the burial chamber of an Anglo-Saxon king (AD 625).

Clocks and watches

The sound of ticking leads you to room 44, full of timepieces. A 1.5m- (5ft-) high carillon clock rings out the hours as it has for 400 years, and the 'Nef', shaped like a galleon, used to pitch and toss, fire guns, blow its trumpets and even tell the time!

'Ginger'

'Ginger', a naturally-preserved 5,300-year-old man, is one of the earliest mummies ever discovered (room 64).

One of the richest and most varied collections of treasures in the world is enclosed within the walls of the magnificent building of the British Museum

Buckingham Palace

The London residence of the Sovereign is on the 'must see' list of every first-time visitor to the capital. Yet, to anyone expecting a fairy-tale palace with turrets and towers, this building is a surprise, even a disappointment. The façade is an early 19th-century statement of grandeur, impressive for its massive scale rather than its opulence. The original house was commissioned by the Duke of Buckingham in 1702, and became a royal residence 60 years later when it was sold to George III.

The transformation of Buckingham House into Buckingham Palace was the work of George IV and his favourite architect, John Nash. Queen Victoria, however, was the first monarch to live permanently in the palace, moving in when she acceded to the throne in 1837. Ten years later the two eastern wings were linked, and the main gateway, Marble Arch, was removed to its present site. The elaborate main gates, bearing the royal coat of arms, were added by Edward VII, along with the Queen Victoria Memorial.

Today, Buckingham Palace is both royal home and office, with some 300 royal household staff. Of the 775 rooms, 19 are open to the public in late summer. These state rooms are rich with colour, with chandeliers and gold decorative work, paintings and precious *objets d'art*. The gardens around cover 16 hectares (40 acres).

The Royal Standard flies over the palace (and the other royal homes) when the Queen is in residence.

The Mall, SW1.
Tel: (020) 7766 7300. www.royal.gov.uk.
Open: daily Aug & Sept 9.45am–6pm, last admission 3.45pm.
Admission charge.
Tube: Victoria, Green Park or Hyde Park Corner.

JOHN NASH (1752–1835)

This architect changed the face of London, thanks to the patronage of George IV, who governed as Prince Regent from 1811 until his accession in 1820. The defeat of Napoleon in 1815 fuelled the prince's desire to turn London into a capital equal to any on the continent. Nash fulfilled this ambition with his master plan. Regent Street, from Waterloo Place to the new Regent's Park, was to be overlooked by terraces of elegant classical houses. Regent's Canal and even Trafalgar Square were part of the plan. The transformation of Buckingham House into a palace was a major commission. Enlarged and made splendid, Nash placed a triumphal arch in front as a royal entrance, and redesigned St James's Park. The Marble Arch was later moved, as it proved too narrow for the State Coach.

Buckingham Palace from St James's Park

The Queen's Gallery
Regular exhibitions allow the public to see one of the finest private collections of art and antiques in the world.
Buckingham Palace Rd, SW1.
Tel: (020) 7766 7301;
www.royalcollection.org.uk.
Open: daily 10am–5.30pm. Closed: 29 Sept–16 Oct, 25 & 26 Dec. Admission charge. Tube: Victoria or St James's Park.

The Royal Mews
The Royal Stables house the Windsor grey horses as well as the carriages used for royal pageantry. Most splendid of all is the 230-year-old Gold State Coach, used for coronations and requiring eight horses to pull it. More romantic is the Glass Coach, seen by millions on television in 1981 when Lady Diana Spencer rode in it for her marriage to the Prince of Wales.
Buckingham Palace Rd, SW1.
Tel: (020) 7766 7302.
www.royalcollection.org.uk. Open: 28 Mar–31 Oct Sat–Thur 11am–4pm; except Aug–Sept 10am–5pm. Closed: State visits. Admission charge.
Tube: Victoria.

Guards Museum
With bright red coats and black bearskin helmets, the guards look theatrical but they are fighting men, as the historical display emphasises, telling the Foot Guards' story from the Crimea to North Africa, and from Waterloo to the Gulf.
Wellington Barracks, Birdcage Walk, SW1. Tel: (020) 7414 3271. www.theguardsmuseum.com. Open: daily 10am–4pm. Closed: Christmas Day. Can close at short notice for ceremonies. Admission charge. Tube: St James's Park.

Loyal greetings
Visitors can sign the Queen's visitors' book. Ask the policeman at the box by the right-hand gate.

The royal connection

The Changing of the Guard

'They're changing guard at Buckingham Palace – Christopher Robin went down with Alice.'

Thousands follow the example of AA Milne's characters to watch the best free show in town. There are ceremonial guard changings at four royal palaces: Buckingham Palace, St James's Palace, Whitehall and Windsor Castle. The best and most dramatic is in the forecourt of Buckingham Palace. Quite simply, the New Guard is relieving the Sovereign's Old Guard.

First, the St James's detachment of the Old Guard marches the Colour from Friary Court, St James's Palace, to join the Buckingham Palace Old Guard between 11am and 11.30am. The New Guard marches from Wellington Barracks to Buckingham Palace where the keys are ceremonially handed over to them at 11.33am. The band plays for about half an hour while the New Guard is briefed.

Once the new sentries are properly posted, the Old Guard marches off to return to Wellington Barracks, the St James's detachment of the New Guard marches up the Mall to St James's Palace, and the New Guard takes over the duties of guarding the Queen at Buckingham Palace for the next 24 hours.

The ceremony takes place every day from May to July, and every other day from August to April. Wet weather may cause cancellation. Check dates and information with *www.royal.gov.uk*

Trooping the Colour

This annual parade takes place on the Queen's Official Birthday on the second Saturday in June, but the original reason for the pomp and circumstance was purely practical. Flags, or 'colours', were the rallying point for troops in the land battles of yesteryear. The colour was, therefore, trooped in front of each unit so that every man would be able to recognise his flag.

The Queen appears both as Sovereign and as Colonel-in-Chief of the seven regiments of the Household Division. Since 1987, she has travelled by carriage rather than side-saddle on horseback. If she is delayed, the clock on Horse Guards Parade is held so that it strikes 11 the moment she arrives!

State opening of Parliament

To open the new parliamentary session in late October/early November, the Queen drives in the Irish Coach, purchased by Queen Victoria

---

THE QUEEN

Queen Elizabeth II (born in 1926) is one of the world's busiest heads of state. During her 57-year reign there have been 11 British prime ministers and 11 US presidents. In a typical year, she will visit 10 countries, attend 75 receptions, preside over 11 meetings of the Privy Council, give 150 audiences and hand out 2,000 medals.

specifically for this procession. Starting at Buckingham Palace, she travels along the Mall, then down Whitehall to the House of Lords, where her arrival is marked by a gun salute.

The Queen's speech, broadcast on television, is a statement of the government's forthcoming plans, and its ritual can be traced back to the 13th century. Back in 1605, Guy Fawkes's Gunpowder Plot aimed to blow up King James I and all who were in attendance. The cellars of the Palace of Westminster are still searched before state openings.

Court Circular

To see the Royal Family in person, read the Court Circular (official engagements) in newspapers like *The Times* and the *Daily Telegraph*.

Royal Warrants

Some 800 of Britain's oldest and most prestigious shops and businesses display Royal Warrants, the coats of arms that mark them as suppliers of goods to royal households, from overcoats to meats to saddles. This official recognition dates back to the 15th century, but the warrant can never be used in blatant advertising, ensuring the personal tastes of the Royal Family remain secret.

The Queen's garden parties

Throughout July, garden parties bring men in their best suits, and ladies wearing hats and smart frocks to Buckingham Palace. Some 8,000 people at a time are invited to stroll on the lawns, listen to the band, and hope for a glimpse of Her Majesty.

The Changing of the Guard, a spectacular ceremonial display

Walk: Royal London

This is the pomp and circumstance route, along the Mall built by Edward VII in honour of his mother, Queen Victoria.

Allow 1 hour.

Start at Charing Cross underground station, cross Trafalgar Square and go through Admiralty Arch.

1 Admiralty Arch and the Mall
The central arch is traditionally reserved for the monarch. Look to the left down Horse Guards Parade: this open space is the site of the annual pageants, Trooping the Colour and Beating the Retreat.

2 Duke of York's Steps
The Duke's statue stands high on a pillar. At the end of the terrace is a sober-looking statue of George VI.

3 St James's Park
Thank Charles II for making this royal enclosure a public park. The 36.4 hectares (90 acres) of lawn, lake and gardens are quieter now than when the 'Merry Monarch' used to bring his mistress and dogs down for a stroll.
Turn right at the traffic lights.

4 Marlborough House and the Queen's Chapel
Designed by Sir Christopher Wren, Marlborough House is home of the Commonwealth Secretariat. Inigo Jones's elegant nearby Queen's Chapel is open for Sunday services.

5 St James's Palace
Five kings and queens have been born in this palace built for Henry VIII and new monarchs are still proclaimed from a balcony. Numerous royal weddings have been celebrated in the Chapel Royal, including Queen Victoria's in 1840.
Cross Marlborough Rd at the George IV gates. Continue along the front of the palace.

6 St James's Palace, Gate House
Sentries guard the gateway of this photogenic Tudor tower, the clock of which bears the initials 'W R' (William IV) and the date 1832.
Follow Cleveland Row to the cul-de-sac. Behind Selwyn House a gate leads to

Green Park. Turn left and follow Queen's Walk back to the Mall.

7 Clarence House

Clarence House is the London home of Prince Charles, his sons William and Harry and the Duchess of Cornwall. *Tel: 020 7766 7303. www. royalcollection.org.uk. Open: Aug–Sept 10am–4pm. Admission charge.*
Turn right on The Mall towards Buckingham Palace.

8 Buckingham Palace

The Victoria Memorial shows a portly, 'unamused' Queen Victoria. Although made grander by George IV, 'Buck House' (as some call it) was first lived in by Queen Victoria. Look closely at the detail on the massive main gates.
Follow the railings to Buckingham Palace Gate. Cross over to Birdcage Walk.

9 Birdcage Walk

This walkway was named after the menagerie of Charles II. On the right, the band forms up before the Changing of the Guard at Wellington Barracks. Further along is the Guards Museum and the Royal Military Chapel.
Turn right on to Queen Anne's Walk and enter Queen Anne's Gate.

10 Queen Anne's Gate

The brick houses in this hidden enclave are all decorated with terracotta heads. Note the ugly faces above the little statue of Queen Anne.
St James's Park underground station is visible down Queen Anne's Gate.

Walk: Royal London

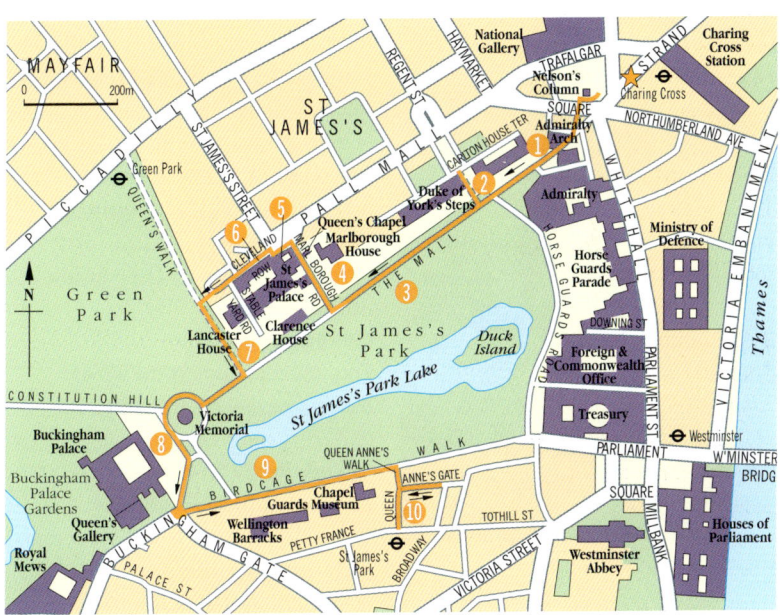

Cabinet War Rooms

Located 3m (10ft) underground, this 21-room maze is kept as it was during World War II bombing raids when it housed Churchill, the War Cabinet and the Chiefs of Staff. A national museum dedicated to the life and times of former PM Winston Churchill was opened in 2005.
Clive Steps, King Charles St, SW1. Tel: (020) 7930 6961. www.iwm.org.uk. Open: daily 9.30am–6pm. Closed: 24–26 Dec. Admission charge. Tube: Westminster.

Camden Town

This is a hip area, famous for its funky shops and weekend market for those who favour alternative fashion. Here you can also take a canal trip from Camden Lock to Little Venice.
London Waterbus, Camden Lock, NW1. Tel: (020) 7482 2550. Open: daily Apr–Sept. Tube: Camden Town.

Carnaby Street, renowned in the 1960s for its fashionable boutiques, has undergone a facelift

Carnaby Street

In the 'Swinging Sixties', this was the street for buying miniskirts and flower-power shirts. By the 1980s, it was jaded and faded, but Carnaby Street, plus neighbouring Foubert's Place, Ganton Street and Newburgh Street, is being revitalised. Once again, it is a fun place to visit.
Carnaby St, W1. Tube: Oxford Circus.

Cartoon Museum

This museum displays the wit of Britain's cartoonists from the 18th century to the present day.
35 Little Russell St, WC1. Tel: (020) 7580 8155. www.cartoonmuseum.org. Open: Tues–Sat 10.30am–5.30pm, Sun noon–5.30pm. Admission charge. Tube: Holborn, Tottenham Court Road.

A statue of King Charles II stands in Chelsea Hospital's central court

Chelsea
See Walk, pp34–5.

Chelsea Hospital
See Royal Hospital, Chelsea, pp34 & 83.

Chiswick
See Walk, pp36–7.

Cleopatra's Needle
Dating from 1450 BC, this 21m (69ft) granite obelisk is London's oldest outdoor monument. Originally a tribute to various Egyptian gods and rulers, it was presented to Britain by the Viceroy of Egypt in 1819, and towed to London behind a boat in 1878.
Victoria Embankment, WC2.
Tube: Embankment.

Courtauld Gallery
Worth visiting for the beautifully restored 18th-century interior alone! Best known are the Impressionist and Post-Impressionist works. Edouard Manet's *Bar at the Folies-Bergère,* and Van Gogh's *Self-Portrait with Bandaged Ear* hang among works by Monet, Cézanne, Gauguin, Degas and Pissarro in the former exhibition room of the Royal Academy.

Other treasures include silver made by the Courtauld forebears, French Huguenot refugees who were silversmiths long before the family business was fabrics; a collection of medieval Italian and Dutch paintings, including a richly coloured triptych dating from 1410 to 1420; a collection of 34,000 Old Master prints and drawings; and 20th-century British painting and sculpture ranging from Sickert to Sutherland. At the top of the building is the Royal Academy of Art Great Room, where Summer Exhibitions were held 200 years ago. (*See also* Somerset House, *p90.*)
Somerset House, The Strand, WC2.
Tel: (020) 7848 2526.
www.courtauld.ac.uk.
Open: daily 10am–6pm. Closed: 25 & 26 Dec. Admission charge.
Tube: Temple (closed Sun), Covent Garden or Holborn.

The mighty Cleopatra's Needle on Victoria Embankment

Walk: Village London: Chelsea

As London grew, it swallowed adjacent villages like Chelsea, whose walled gardens and elegant houses have always attracted artists and writers.

Allow at least 1½ hours.

Start at Sloane Square underground station. Exit and go straight ahead towards Peter Jones department store and the King's Rd.

1 King's Road
The 'Swinging Sixties' launched the King's Road internationally, and some of its shops are still fashionable despite incursions by familiar chain stores.
Continue past the new Saatchi Gallery and turn left on Royal Ave.

2 Royal Hospital
Beyond the sports fields of Burton Court, the Royal Hospital houses over 400 'pensioners', old soldiers who wear the distinctive scarlet coat.
Turn right on St Leonard's Terrace.

3 St Leonard's Terrace
Bram Stoker, creator of Dracula, lived at No 18, one of a series of handsome Georgian houses. Turn left into Tedworth Square and on to the corner of Tite Street where Mark Twain lived (1896–7). Further down Tite Street, across Royal Hospital Road, Oscar Wilde moved into No 34 with his wife Constance Lloyd. Painter John Singer Sargent lived and died at No 31.
Turn right on Dilke St, and right again into Swan Walk.

4 Chelsea Physic Garden
There are 6,000 species in this study garden founded by the Worshipful Society of Apothecaries in 1673.
Follow Swan Walk to Royal Hospital Rd and turn left. Cheyne Walk bends to the right just before the Embankment.

5 Cheyne Walk
Cheyne Walk is the poshest address in Chelsea. Until the Embankment was built in 1874 it looked right over the Thames. George Eliot moved into No 4 in 1880, only to die three weeks later. More recently Rolling Stone Keith Richards lived at No 3. Notice the gates of Pre-Raphaelite painter Dante Gabriel Rossetti's house, No 16.

Beyond Oakley Street, Mick Jagger once lived at No 48 in a surprisingly prim house, while painter Whistler spent time at Lindsey House (Nos 96–100), beyond Beaufort Street, built in 1674.
Turn right on Cheyne Row, past the King's Head & Eight Bells pub.

6 Carlyle's House
No 24, dating from 1708, was Thomas Carlyle's home from 1834–81.
Turn left on Upper Cheyne Row and left again on Lawrence St. Turn right, past the Cross Keys pub.

7 Chelsea Old Church
The church is associated with Henry VIII's ill-fated chancellor, Sir Thomas More, whose statue sits outside. Note the kneelers, needlework remembrances of those who have worshipped here in the past 700 years.
Turn right up Old Church St.

8 Old Church Street
At No 46, hand-painted tiles and huge cows' heads mark the site of a Victorian dairy.
Continue to the King's Rd, cross over and catch a bus back to Sloane Square.

Walk: Village London: Chiswick and Hammersmith

Chiswick, some 10km (6 miles) west of Piccadilly Circus, has fine houses and Hammersmith has good riverside pubs. In fine weather, this is well worth the 30-minute Tube journey.

Allow 1½ hours.

From Turnham Green underground station (note that the Piccadilly Line does not often stop here) turn left, and at the traffic lights cross Chiswick High Rd. Turn right and immediately left into Devonshire Rd. The street ends at the Hogarth roundabout. By the Feathers pub, go down the pedestrian subway, turning right half-way along. Re-emerge and keep to the right of the office block; 200m (220yds) on is Hogarth's House.

1 Hogarth's House
Back in the 18th century, painter William Hogarth considered this a country 'box by the Thames'. Inside are many of his satirical engravings.
Continue on Hogarth Lane and take the first entrance to Chiswick House. Follow the avenue and turn right.

2 Chiswick House
Built in 1729, this Palladian-style villa was designed largely by wealthy arts patron Lord Burlington. This elegant backdrop for his collection of paintings and sculptures has been restored to its 18th-century style, as have the William Kent gardens.
Go around the house and exit on Burlington Lane. Turn left, cross the road, and continue to the roundabout.

3 Chiswick Square
The handsome Boston House dominates the square where Becky Sharp hurled 'Johnson's Dixonary... back into the garden' in Thackeray's *Vanity Fair*.
Turn right into Church St.

4 Church Street
This is Old Chiswick, which still feels like a rural retreat. The Old Burlington, once a pub, supposedly served infamous highwayman Dick Turpin's wedding breakfast.
At the church, turn right, and circle anti-clockwise.

5 Chiswick Parish Church
St Nicholas's dates back 800 years. Local lore insists that the headless

body of Oliver Cromwell was buried with his daughter, Mary, in the Fauconberg vault. The architect and landscape gardener William Kent, and painter JM Whistler, are buried in the graveyard. On the river side of the church is the imposing tomb of Hogarth, inscribed with a moving tribute by the actor David Garrick.
Leave the churchyard by the steps leading to Chiswick Mall.

6 Chiswick Mall

This is one of London's prettiest streets, with grand houses on the left, and the River Thames, gardens and houseboats on the right. Behind Red Lion House is the 300-year-old Griffin Brewery where Fuller's beers are brewed. Still tidal here, the Thames regularly floods the street. Walpole House is said to be Miss Pinkerton's Academy in *Vanity Fair*.

Continue along the river, past Hammersmith Terrace.

7 Riverside pubs

The Black Lion pub is the first of many popular riverside pubs. Patrons of the Old Ship can spill out into the gardens, while, further on, past William Morris's old home at 26 Upper Mall, is the Dove, a pub with bags of history. Graham Greene and Ernest Hemingway drank here, and James Thomson, the author of *Rule, Britannia*, died upstairs.

Past the gardens, the Rutland and the Blue Anchor cater to the rowing fraternity from neighbouring boathouses and clubs.
Walk under Hammersmith Bridge and immediately turn left on to Hammersmith Bridge Rd which leads back to Hammersmith underground station.

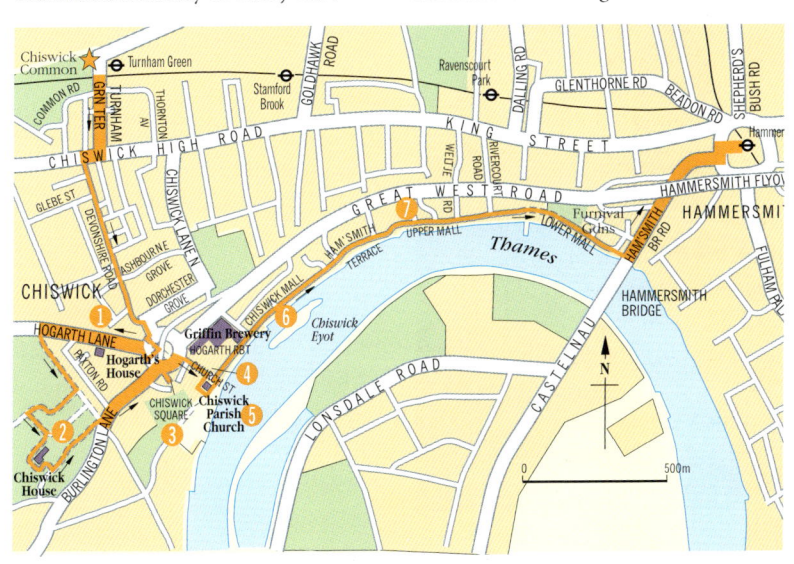

Churches

London's churches are more than just places of worship. They are also part of the city's heritage. With fewer people living in the city centre, congregations have dwindled, but that does not mean the churches are merely museums.

Many people visit London's churches solely for the music. Regular concerts are held in, and broadcast from, churches like St John's, Smith Square and All Souls, Langham Place. St Martin-in-the-Fields on Trafalgar Square has regular free lunchtime concerts, and also attracts people to the popular, inexpensive restaurant in the crypt. It is also home to the London Brass Rubbing Centre currently undergoing a £36 million restoration project.

In the City, office workers enjoy lunchtime dialogues at St Mary-le-Bow on Cheapside, when the rector discusses a topic with a distinguished guest.

The Samaritans are a non-religious movement, but this international organisation, offering a 24-hour telephone helpline, was the brainchild of the rector of St Stephen Walbrook. Its offices moved to larger premises in 1987, but the original telephone 'for listening, not preaching' rests on a plinth in the church.

Churches also offer respite from the noise of city traffic and the stress of crowds, enabling visitors, shoppers and workers to recharge their batteries with a few minutes' peace . . . and, if they wish, prayer.

The white spire of St Clement Danes

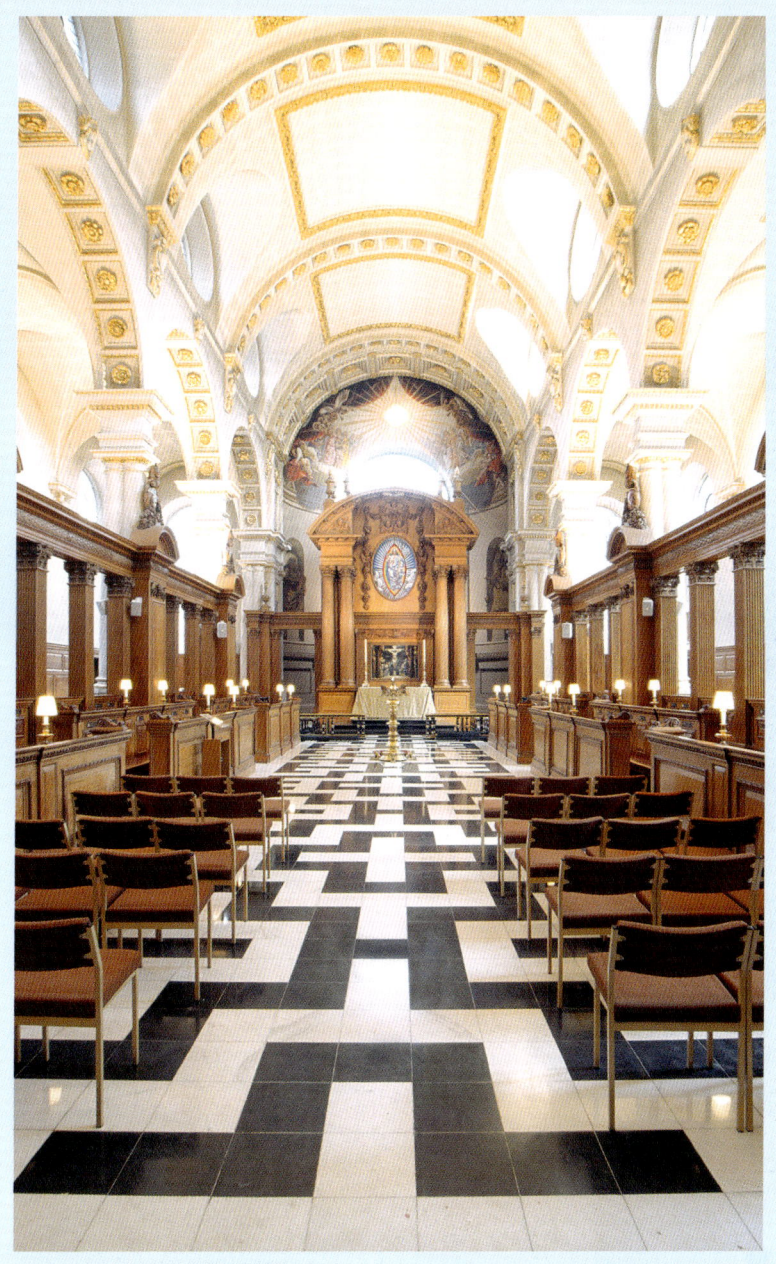

St Bride's, Fleet Street: for 500 years, the spiritual home of journalists and printers

London churches

London's churches range from tiny chapels to the world-famous St Paul's Cathedral and Westminster Abbey (see pp86–7 and 110–11). In the City alone there are churches dating from almost every century since Christianity was established in Britain more than 1,400 years ago.

Only eight churches survived the Great Fire of 1666 and, of the 89 destroyed, Sir Christopher Wren rebuilt 51. More restoration was needed after World War II. Most churches close around 7pm. They are generally open to the public free of charge. There are hundreds of churches all over London, but the following give a flavour of the development of architecture and design.

Seventh century: All Hallows by the Tower, whose Saxon archway was built with Roman tiles, provided grandstand viewing for Samuel Pepys to watch the Great Fire.
Byward St, EC3. Tel: (020) 7481 2928. www.allhallowsbythetower.org.uk. Open: Mon–Fri 8am–6pm, Sat & Sun 10am–5pm (closed during services).

Twelfth century: In **St Bartholomew-the-Great**, solid Norman columns and arches recall the Augustinian monks who walked through the 14th-century cloisters (now renovated).
West Smithfield, EC1. Tel: (020) 7606 5171. www.greatstbarts.com. Open: 15 Feb–10 Nov Mon–Fri 8.30am–5pm, Sat 10.30am–4pm, Sun 8.30am–8pm; 11 Nov–14 Feb 8.30am–4pm. Admission charge.

St Helen's, Bishopsgate, is a rare survivor of the Great Fire, and exemplifies the medieval love of monuments and funerary effigies.

SIR CHRISTOPHER WREN (1632–1723)

A brilliant astronomer, mathematician and engineer, Wren was appointed King Charles II's Surveyor-General in 1669 following the Great Fire. Unfortunately his master plan for a new London was defeated by a complex network of land ownership and a lack of funds. His churches were designed specifically for a congregation to see and hear the preacher clearly. Soaring spires, black-and-white tiled floors, wooden box-pews, plain walls and clear glass windows characterise his churches. Other Wren projects range from work on Hampton Court Palace to the Sheldonian Theatre in Oxford.

Great St Helen's, Bishopsgate, EC3.
Tel: (020) 7283 2231.
www.st-helens.org.uk.
Open: Mon–Fri 9am–5pm.

Thirteenth century: St Etheldreda's is a fine example of Gothic architecture. Little else remains of the once-impressive Palace of the Bishop of Ely.
14 Ely Place, EC1. Tel: (020) 7405 1061.
Open: daily 7.30am–6.30pm.

Fifteenth century: St Olave's: 'A country church in the world of Seething Lane', according to former Poet Laureate John Betjeman. Samuel Pepys is buried here.
8 Hart St, EC3. Tel: (020) 7488 4318.
Open: Mon–Fri 10am–4pm.

Sixteenth century: St Andrew Undershaft, of typical English Perpendicular design, was 'improved' by the Victorians, but was damaged by an IRA bomb in 1992.
St Mary Axe, off Leadenhall St, EC3.
Tel: (020) 7283 2231.
Open: by arrangement.

Early 17th century: St Katharine Cree is a rare example of early Renaissance style. Purcell, Handel and Wesley all played on the church organ.
Leadenhall St, EC3. Tel: (020) 7488 4318.
www.sanctuaryinthecity.net.
Open: weekdays 10am–4pm.

Late 17th century: St Mary Abchurch retains a real feel of Wren. The building is square, with a painted dome, and boasts a Grinling Gibbons carving behind the altar.
Abchurch Lane, off Cannon St, EC4.
Tel: (020) 7626 4481. Open: Mon–Thur 10.30am–2pm.

Eighteenth century: St Mary Woolnoth. By Nicholas Hawksmoor, Wren's clerk and pupil, it is baroque, with a rusticated façade and richly ornamented exterior north wall, complemented by lavish interior plasterwork.
Lombard St, EC3. Tel: (020) 7626 9701.
Open: weekdays 7.45am–5pm.

Nineteenth century: St Dunstan-in-the-West. This neo-Gothic church has a clock with bell-striking figures and a statue of Queen Elizabeth.
Fleet St, EC4. Tel: (020) 7405 1929.
www.stdunstaninthewest.org.
Open: Tue 11am–3pm.

Battersea Old Church, south of the river

The City

The Romans founded Londinium. The wall they built, dating from AD 200, set the city limits for over 1,300 years. The City has received special privileges from the Crown since the reign of William the Conqueror. Monastic orders and merchants thrived, adventurers returned with treasure, and Flemish, Jewish and French refugees made the City international.

History

By the 17th century, living conditions were cramped and unsanitary. The Great Plague of 1665 wiped out one-third of the citizens, and the Great Fire, a year later, destroyed 80 per cent of the buildings. Wren's imaginative urban renewal project was impractical, but his plans for St Paul's Cathedral were reluctantly accepted.

Although Westminster had the power of Parliament and the Monarchy, the Industrial Revolution and a burgeoning Empire made the City the world centre of finance. In the 19th century, the resident population dwindled as trains and the efficient bus network enabled workers to commute from greener districts. Today, of London's 7.5 million, a mere 8,000 call the City 'home'. World War II bombing and continuing redevelopment have changed the face of the City. Now, glass and steel canyons overshadow landmarks such as the Bank of England, the Royal Exchange and Mansion House.

The Lord Mayor

On the second Saturday of November, the Lord Mayor of London parades through the City in a golden coach drawn by six massive shire horses. For almost 800 years this procession (*www.lordmayorsshow.org*) has been held, as the Mayor rides to the Queen's Bench, Royal Courts of Justice to pledge allegiance to the Crown. The position of Lord Mayor is mainly ceremonial. It is an elected office with a term of one year.

DICK WHITTINGTON – THE REALITY AND THE LEGEND

Dick Whittington and his cat make a popular fairy-tale of rags to riches. Yet Sir Richard was real. A stone on Highgate Hill recalls the spot where Dick is supposed to have heard Bow Bells (some 6km/3¾ miles away!) ring out 'Turn again, Whittington, thrice Lord Mayor of London'. He did, made a fortune, gave enormous sums to charity, and was four times Mayor between 1397 and 1419.

Detail from the Royal Exchange, dating from the 19th century

Finance
'A man's word is his bond' is the City's age-old slogan from the early days of trading. The Royal Exchange, founded by Sir Thomas Gresham, provided a focus for merchants from the late 16th century, but the other main financial institutions date from a century later. The Bank of England, set up to finance the war with France in 1694, was soon banker to the government and the entire banking system.

Coffee houses became centres for deals to be made. 'Brokers' and 'jobbers' met in places such as Jonathan's Coffee House in Change Alley, to buy and sell stocks for clients. Merchants, ship owners and sea captains congregating in Edward Lloyd's Coffee House in Lombard Street, were the forerunners of Lloyd's of London's multi-million pound insurance business.

The Baltic Exchange building, in St Mary's Axe, was damaged extensively by an IRA bomb in 1992 and then dismantled; the Baltic Exchange company, in a new St Mary's Axe location, handles much of the world's cargo movements today. In the old days, deals were sealed with a handshake, and the words: 'my word is my bond' were taken at face value; in today's high-tech world, negotiations are conducted more remotely – via satellite, electronic mail, computer printout or facsimile.

Culture and education
Few children now live in the City, but the famous City of London School (established 1834) and the City of London School for Girls (in the Barbican) attract pupils from all over the capital. These, like the Guildhall School of Music and Drama and City University, come under the responsibility of the Corporation of London.

The Barbican Centre, opened by Queen Elizabeth in 1982, is home to the London Symphony Orchestra, and also has an art gallery, a conference centre and two exhibition halls. Nearby, the Museum of London tells the story of the capital.

Nearby attractions
Financial London walk (*see pp46–7*)
Saints and Sinners walk (*see pp48–9*)
Barbican Centre (*see p23*)
Guildhall (*see p60*)
Lloyd's of London (*see p47, p66*)
Mansion House (*see p71*)
St Paul's Cathedral (*see pp86–7*)

The City

The square mile of the City of London boasts 2,000 years of history and 800 years of pageantry and tradition, but these are only a backdrop for the dynamic business world of the City today.

On weekdays, the City (always with a capital C) buzzes with over 300,000 office workers. Revolving around the Stock Exchange, the City is one of the world's three largest financial centres, a convenient five hours ahead of New York and nine hours behind Tokyo. Some 500 banks from 70 countries have branches here.

Everywhere deals are being made: in insurance at Lloyd's, in shipping on the Baltic Exchange, in commodities, metals and financial futures. The City

An aerial view of the City

is an international marketplace where money is the common language, cut-throat competition thrives, and fortunes are made and lost.

These cosmopolitan workers can relax in 180 tiny parks and gardens, listen to music in ancient churches, drink in Victorian pubs, play squash in a high-tech sports club or imbibe culture at the Barbican Centre. Opened in 1982, 'The City's gift to the nation' is home to the London Symphony Orchestra.

The recent financial maelstrom has shaken, but not destroyed, the Square Mile. London has survived fire, floods and bombs; it is the most resilient of cities.

Guildhall, City of London

Walk: Financial London

An international financial centre for over 300 years, the City developed through gentlemen meeting and doing business in taverns and coffee houses.

Allow 2 hours.

Start at Mansion House underground station. Turn right to Queen Victoria St.

1 Queen Victoria Street
Here, the ancient and modern stand side by side. There are banks, a Victorian fish restaurant at No 39, and accessed from Cannon Street are the ruins of a Roman temple.
Turn right on Bucklersbury to see St Stephen Walbrook. Christopher Wren lived opposite at No 15. Retrace your steps, and cross Queen Victoria St on Bucklersbury to reach Cheapside, then turn left.

2 Cheapside
Once a medieval marketplace. On the opposite side, an iron head with a bishop's mitre marks the supposed birthplace of St Thomas à Becket in 1118.

3 St Mary-Le-Bow
Site of a church since Saxon times, this was built by Wren. For 500 years the bell tolled curfews, hence the saying that true Cockneys (Londoners) had to be born 'within the sound of Bow Bells'.
Cross Cheapside and follow Milk St to Gresham St. Cross in front of St Lawrence Jewry and turn right under the archway to the Guildhall.

4 Guildhall
The administrative powerhouse of the City for over 800 years, the current building dates from 1439.
Leave Guildhall Yard for Gresham St. Turn left and cross the street. Turn right down Ironmonger Lane and cut left through St Olave's Court to Old Jewry. Turn right, and turn left on to Poultry. Cross Prince's St to Threadneedle St and the square in front of the Royal Exchange.

5 Mansion House, the Bank of England and the Royal Exchange
The Duke of Wellington's statue is surrounded by three of the City's most important buildings. To his left is the Lord Mayor of London's official home, Mansion House; to his right is the Bank

of England, the 'Old Lady of Threadneedle Street'; and behind is the Royal Exchange.

Walk along Threadneedle St and turn right behind the Royal Exchange. Pass the bust of PJ Reuter, cross Cornhill and turn left, then right into Ball Court.

6 Meeting places

Simpson's Tavern was established in 1757. Follow Castle Court to the pink Jamaica Wine House, built on the site of London's first coffee house.

Leave the alleys by Bell Inn Yard. Cross Fenchurch St, turn left and go through Leadenhall Market. Exit and look left.

7 Lloyd's of London

London's world-famous insurance business began in Edward Lloyd's coffee house 300 years ago. Today's brokers work in Richard Rogers' space-age building.

Turn right down Lime St and cross Fenchurch St. Continue on Philpot Lane, cross Eastcheap, and head along Botolph Lane. Turn right on to Monument St.

8 The Monument

The 1666 Great Fire of London began in Pudding Lane, 62m (68yds) away from the commemorative column. On the 320th anniversary of the fire in 1986 the Company of Bakers apologised to the Lord Mayor of London for the disaster which began in the shop of Thomas Faryner, the king's baker.

Continue on Monument St to King William St, and turn right to Monument underground station.

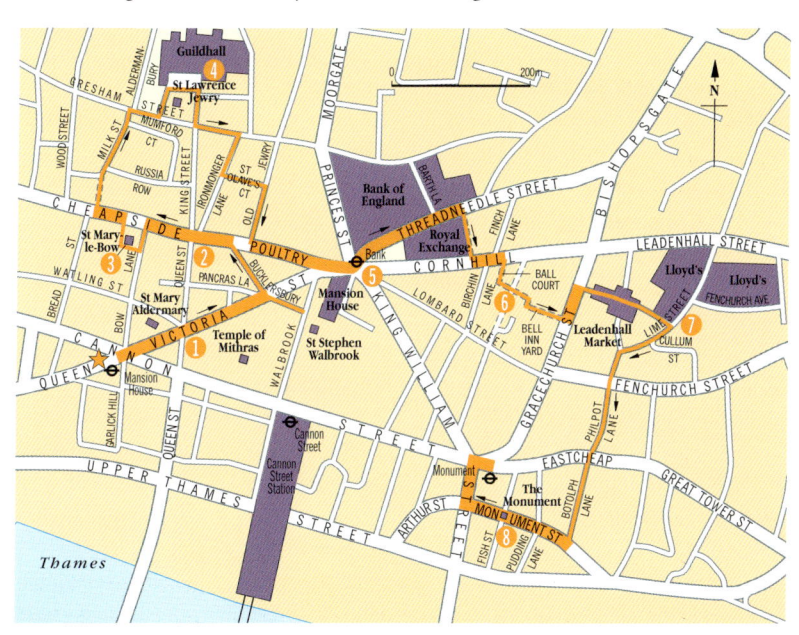

Walk: Saints and sinners

In the City, narrow alleys follow ancient rights of way and lead to pubs and churches hidden in courtyards.

Allow 2 hours.

Start at Blackfriars underground station. Take exit 1 to Queen Victoria St.

1 The Black Friar Pub

A 1903 art nouveau gem on the site of a Dominican priory, the interior is decorated with bronze, marble and mosaic pictures.
Walk up Queen Victoria St. Turn left on to St Andrew's Hill, past the Church of St Andrew-by-the-Wardrobe, rebuilt by Wren in 1695. Turn right on to Carter Lane, and right again under a low arch.

2 Wardrobe Place

The site of the Royal Wardrobe, where kings kept their robes of state.
Return to Carter Lane. Turn left on to Dean's Court, and cross Ludgate Hill for Ave Maria Lane.

3 Ave Maria Lane

On the left is Stationers' Hall whose guild members monopolised book publishing. Illegal books were burnt where a giant plane tree now thrives.
Turn left on to Newgate St and left again on to Old Bailey.

4 Old Bailey

The Central Criminal Court is nicknamed the Old Bailey, after the street. For a gruesome reminder that this was once Newgate Prison, read the plaque on the side of the Magpie and Stump pub.
Return to the crossroads, crossing Holborn Viaduct to St Sepulchre's Church.

5 St Sepulchre's Church

The church was once connected to Newgate Prison by a tunnel, and before executions, a handbell (still in the church) was rung with the chant: 'All you that in the condemned hold do lie, Prepare you, for tomorrow you shall die.'
Continue up Giltspur St, past a memorial to essayist Charles Lamb.

6 Pie Corner

At the corner of Cock Lane a small, fat, golden cherub marks the spot where the Great Fire of London was stopped. A plaque tells a tale of bodysnatchers. *Cross over to St Bartholomew's Hospital.*

7 Smithfield

Smithfield has seen more than its fair share of riots, fairs and executions. The famous St Bartholomew's Fair was held on the site for 700 years, but the most famous incident was the stabbing of a Peasant's Revolt leader by the Lord Mayor in front of King Richard II. Opposite Smithfield is St Bartholomew's hospital. *Continue past the hospital. Go through a half-timbered archway.*

8 St Bartholomew-the-Great

This Norman church dates back to the 12th century. *Admission charge.*

Leave by the side gate and return to West Smithfield on Cloth Fair.

9 Smithfield Market

Still Europe's largest wholesale meat market. The action starts early and is all over by 8am.
Walk through on Grand Ave. Turn left on to Charterhouse St. Cross Farringdon Rd and continue to Ely Place. Turn right.

10 Ely Place

One of London's secret cul-de-sacs, hiding the church of St Etheldreda with its stunning stained-glass west window. *Turn up the narrow alley past Ye Olde Mitre pub. Turn left on Hatton Garden to Holborn. Turn right, and continue to Chancery Lane underground station.*

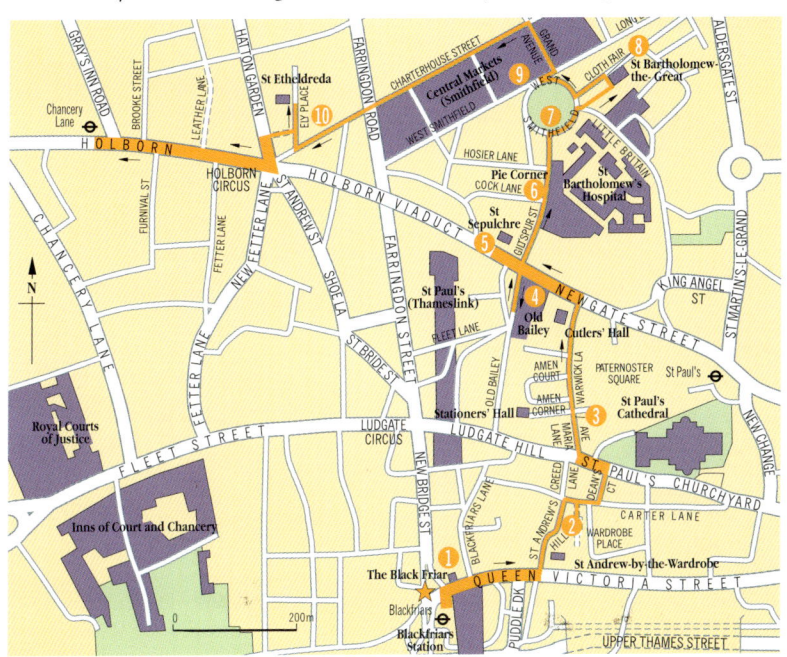

Covent Garden

Eliza Doolittle sold her flowers under the portico of St Paul's Church before Professor Higgins made her his 'Fair Lady'. The portico is still there, as are the elegant buildings that housed London's famous fruit and vegetable market until 1974. Originally a convent garden of 16 hectares (40 acres) belonging to the monks of Westminster Abbey, Inigo Jones built a piazza here in the 1630s, modelled on those he had seen in Italy.

The square, and the covered walks in front of the buildings, attracted market traders from far and wide, and it grew into the most important fruit and vegetable market in the country. The present market buildings were built into the piazza in 1830. Since 1980 the colonnades have echoed to the sound of street entertainment and shopping. A mixture of speciality shops and stalls, old pubs and new wine bars welcome millions of visitors annually to buy fashion and flowers, arts, crafts, books and baubles. There is a market selling antiques on Monday, and crafts from Tuesday to Sunday.

The liveliness has spread into the surrounding streets, such as Long Acre, Neal Street and the charming countrified Neal's Yard.

Nearby attractions
London Transport Museum (*see p70*)
Royal Opera House (*see p148*)

The old Covent Garden market building is now home to a range of shops, pubs and wine bars

The cafés in the interior are very popular

Dickens' London

CHARLES DICKENS (1812–70)

This famous writer and crusader was moulded in early life by his father's humiliating bankruptcy and imprisonment, and his own brief period of working long hours in a blacking factory. He attacked the misery and poverty underlying the world's leading industrial nation, using realistic detail to prick the reader's conscience and larger-than-life characters to tug unashamedly at the heartstrings.

Young Dickens

Dickens' parents were married at St Mary-le-Strand Church (Strand, WC2) opposite Somerset House where his father worked in the Navy Pay Office before being sent to Marshalsea Prison, Southwark. The gaol experience is recalled in *Little Dorrit*, and Mr Micawber is modelled on Dickens Senior.

Charles would have walked down Borough High Street in Southwark to visit him, passing coaching inns that he later described in his books. Only the George Inn (George Inn Yard, SE1), which was mentioned in *Little Dorrit*, remains. The eponymous heroine was christened in the Church of St George the Martyr, further down the road, where she is commemorated in a stained-glass window.

Life improved for Charles when, aged 15, he became a clerk at Ellis and Blackmore lawyers at No 1 South Square (Gray's Inn, WC1). In *David Copperfield*, he placed Traddles and his young wife, Sophy, in the house next door at No 2.

His first short story, *A Dinner at Poplar Walk*, appeared in a magazine in 1833, and more short stories, or 'sketches', followed under the pen-name of Boz. During 1836 *Pickwick Papers* was published (at first in serial form), and Dickens was then affluent enough to marry Catherine Hogarth at St Luke's Church, Chelsea.

Family life

Dickens and his family moved into 48 Doughty Street, WC1, now the Dickens Museum, full of memorabilia, and the only one of his London homes that still stands. Here he finished *Pickwick Papers*. The desk on which he wrote is in the study. Upstairs, Dickens held his sister-in-law, Mary Hogarth, in his arms as she lay dying, aged only 17, a scene recreated with Little Nell in *The Old Curiosity Shop*. There is an 'Old Curiosity Shop' (on Portsmouth Street, WC2) dating from Dickens' time, but there is some conjecture as to whether or not it is the same one referred to in his story.

Dickens, the public figure

As his fame grew, Dickens became a major personality. He frequently visited Thomas Carlyle in Chelsea at 24 Cheyne Row, SW3, and was a founding member of the Arts Club at 40 Dover Street, W1, when it opened in 1863.

Many people and places he knew appeared in his stories. In *Bleak House*, Mr Tulkinghorn's house was based on the home of his biographer, John Forster, at 58 Lincoln's Inn Fields. His career as a reader began here; in his later years, Dickens embarked on an exhausting series of public readings, and toured America in 1867. The awareness of injustice never left him, and in 1859 he started a protest magazine, *All the Year Round*, which he published from a building on the corner of Wellington Street and Tavistock Street, WC2. He died in 1870, aged 58, having worked himself too hard, and is buried in Poets' Corner, Westminster Abbey.

Eating and drinking

Like many of his characters, Dickens enjoyed the social life of taverns and chop houses, many of which still exist. Rules (*see p164*) is known for its Victorian style. The author supposedly ate in a booth at the rear of the first floor. The George and Vulture Restaurant (*3 Castle Court, off Cornhill, EC3. Tel: (020) 7626 9710*), Ye Olde Cheshire Cheese (*see p174*) and the Grapes (*see p174*) were all establishments frequented by Dickens. The Dickens Inn at St Katharine Dock, E1, however, is a newly built 'old' inn: the author's great-grandson was involved in its construction, but that is the only Dickens connection it can rightfully claim.

CHARLES DICKENS MUSEUM
48 Doughty St, WC1. Tel: (020) 7405 2127.
www.dickensmuseum.com.
Open: Mon–Sat 10am–5pm, Sun 11am–5pm.
Admission charge. Tube: Chancery Lane or Russell Square.

The Charles Dickens Museum includes the desk on which he wrote his masterpieces

Docklands

The fastest-changing area of London is east of the City, along the Thames from Tower Bridge, down into the Isle of Dogs where the river forms a huge loop, and continuing on downstream to Woolwich. The population of this 22sq km (8sq mile) area is about 100,000. Offices, shops, restaurants and flats are new or in converted warehouses. The Docklands Light Railway (DLR) connects with the underground network. There are even city farms and a dry-ski slope.

The docks
From the 17th century, the docks were the base of London's worldwide trading network, and had huge warehouses. Smuggling was rife; those caught risked being tied to a post at Execution Dock and drowned as the tide rushed in.

The West India, Royal Victoria and Royal Albert docks were the largest in the world in the 1950s. By 1982 all had been closed.

Wapping
Just east of Tower Bridge is Wapping, where Docklands' most famous pub, the Prospect of Whitby, has fine river views; more genuine is the nearby Town of Ramsgate. Not far away is Tobacco Dock, where former rum and tobacco warehouses are now a factory outlet shopping mall. Across The Highway is St George-in-the-East, built by Nicholas Hawksmoor between 1714–1729.

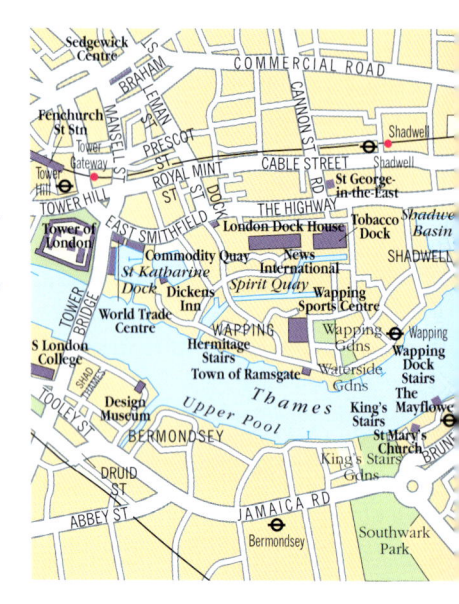

Limehouse
In 1820, this basin linked the docks with the inland canal network. Right on the river is the Grapes, a pub described by Dickens in *Our Mutual Friend*. Next to Commercial Road is St Anne's, another Hawksmoor church, with a clock face from the makers of the face of Big Ben.

Large Chinese communities settled here long before Soho became London's Chinatown.

Isle of Dogs
The reflective glass-covered office blocks here could be transplants from North American cities, but the Ledger Building, Dockmaster's House, Sugar Warehouse and Cannon Workshops, once home to coopers (barrel-makers), are reminders of the past. All, however,

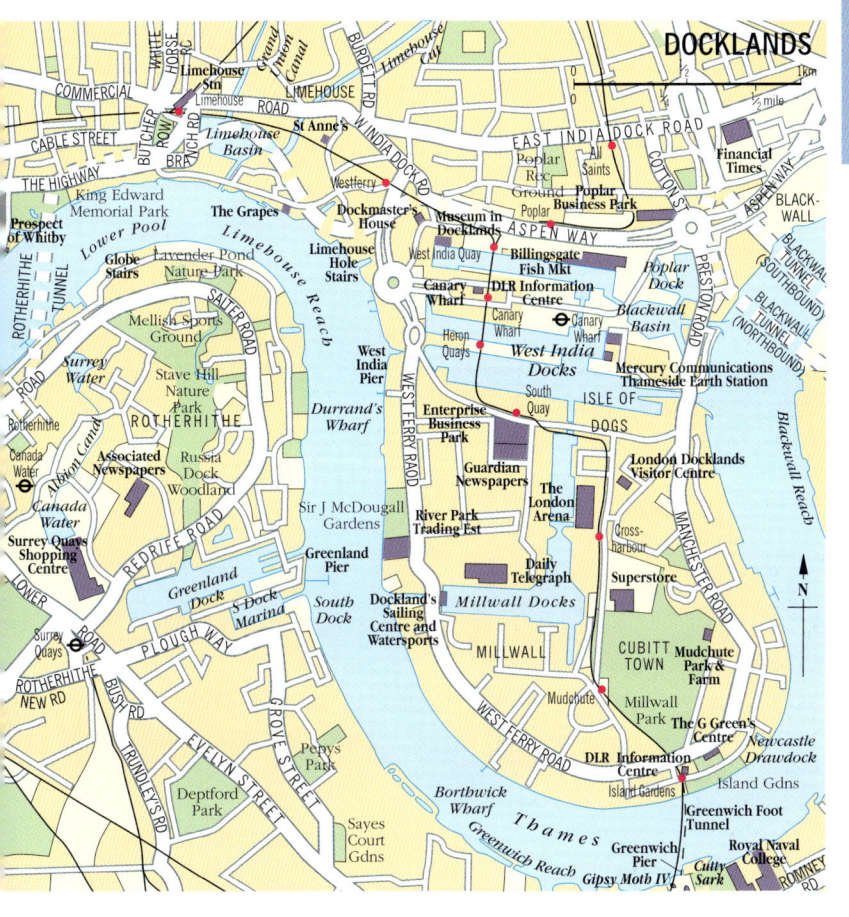

are dwarfed by Canary Wharf Tower which can be seen from miles away. At the southern tip of the Isle of Dogs are the green havens of Mudchute Farm and Island Gardens, with a foot tunnel to Greenwich.

South of the river

Near Tower Bridge is Shad Thames, the old maze of warehouses linked by high-level walkways. Nearby, Butler's Wharf houses the Design Museum (*28 Shad Thames, SE1. Tel: 020 7403 6933*). Further downstream, a little of old Rotherhithe remains. The Mayflower pub dates back to 1550; from here the *Mayflower* sailed off in 1620 to take the Pilgrims to the New World. A memorial to its skipper, Captain Jones, is in St Mary's Church. A bonus in travelling on the Docklands Light Railway (*www.tfl.gov.uk/dlr*) is the superb views from the elevated track.

Ethnic London

In 1870, Prime Minister Disraeli described London as 'a nation, not a city'. Today, London is a complete mixture of races, creeds and colours. This international port and former capital of the Empire has always been multicultural, but since the Norman invasion back in 1066, newcomers have been immigrants, rather than conquerors.

The Notting Hill Carnival celebrates London's multiculturalism

London's Chinatown in Soho, decorated for Chinese New Year

Street names like Old Jewry and Lombard Street recall medieval Jewish and Italian merchants and bankers. The 17th century brought the French Huguenots, Protestants fleeing Catholic France. More recent émigrés have come from the old Empire, the new Commonwealth and from other EU countries: from the Caribbean and Africa, Cyprus and Hong Kong, Pakistan and India, Australia and New Zealand and Eastern Europe.

Foreign festivals have become London festivals, from dragon dancers in Chinatown for the Chinese New Year, to the Caribbean-style Notting Hill Carnival at the end of August.

Foreign cuisines have widened the restaurant choice. Londoners can now eat food from Vietnam, Brazil and Ethiopia; they sip Italian cappuccino and nibble French pastries in cafés, and drink retsina in transplanted Greek tavernas; they pop to Brick Lane for a delicious curry dish.

While Americans play softball in Hyde Park, films of Irish hurling are shown in a Hammersmith cinema, and the mosque in Regent's Park calls faithful Muslims to prayer.

London absorbs them all and benefits from their traditions. They may start out as immigrants, but they all eventually end up as Londoners.

Design Museum
See p103.

Downing Street
Just as the White House is metonymic with the President of the United States, so No 10 Downing Street is always linked to the Prime Minister. Number 10 has been the home of British prime ministers since 1732, but only in 1989, on the orders of Margaret Thatcher, were gates erected at the end of this short cul-de-sac of 300-year-old houses. Linked internally with No 11 (home of the Chancellor of the Exchequer) and No 12 (formerly the home of the Chief Whip), No 10 looks modest enough from the front, but leads to a large complex of offices at the rear.
Tube: Westminster or Charing Cross.

Fleet Street
Fleet Street has been synonymous with printing and publishing for 500 years. Linking the City and the lawyers of the Inns of Court, the street was full of scribes and clerks until Wynkyn de Worde set up his printing press near St Bride's Church in 1500. The industry boomed. In 1702, the *Daily Courant*, Britain's first daily paper, was published

The modest yet elegant doorway of Number 10 Downing Street

THE THUNDERER
Although it is neither the oldest nor the bestselling newspaper in Britain, *The Times* is the most famous. Known as *The Thunderer* since 1831, when a leader (editorial) 'thundered' for Parliamentary reform, its views have carried weight on national and international issues. The views of its readers, however, are equally influential. Letters to the Editor come from people at the top of their field.

Tradition is important to the newspaper. It was founded in 1785 by John Walter, whose descendants were proprietors until 1966. In that year a major change occurred: the front page carried the news! Before that, it had always carried advertisements. More changes took place after 1981, when this pillar of the establishment was bought by Rupert Murdoch, whose media empire included the tabloid newspaper *The Sun*. In 2004 *The Times* also became tabloid (or compact).

at Ludgate Circus. When, in 1986, the News International group moved *The Times, The Sun, News of the World* and the *Sunday Times* to Docklands, the former 'Street of Ink' dried up. Now there are few reminders of the street's colourful past – merely the smoky atmosphere of a journalists' haunt, El Vino's wine bar, and the local museum of history in St Bride's, designed by Wren, and known as the journalists' church.

Geffrye Museum

This row of Grade I-listed 18th-century almshouses contains English living room interiors dating from 1600 to the present day. They reflect the taste and style of the period, from Elizabethan oak-panelling to refined Georgian, cluttered Victorian, 1930s art deco and contemporary 1950s 'modern' loft-style.
Kingsland Rd, E2. Tel: (020) 7739 9893.
www.geffrye-museum.org.uk.
Open: Tue–Sat 10am–5pm, Sun & Bank Holidays noon–5pm. Free admission.
Tube: Liverpool St or Old St, then take a bus.

Gray's Inn

One of the four Inns of Court, lawyers have practised here for 600 years. Few old buildings survived the bombs of World War II. An exception is No 1 South Square (1759) where Charles Dickens worked as a clerk in 1827. Shakespeare's *Comedy of Errors* might have been first performed in the Hall. Its 16th-century screen is reputedly

Gray's Inn – established in the 14th century

carved from the wood of a galleon captured from the Spanish Armada.

The gardens of the Inn, originally laid out by Sir Francis Bacon, and known as the Walks, are open to the public.
Open: Mon–Fri noon–2.30pm.
Tube: Chancery Lane.

Guildhall

The 'town hall' for the City of London, the Guildhall has been the seat of local government for over 800 years. The crypt, porch and walls date from 1411. Names of Lord Mayors are in the Great Hall, along with coats of arms of the guilds and banners of the 12 great livery companies. Mythical giants Gog and Magog guard the Musicians' Gallery. They replaced earlier statues that were destroyed in the Blitz.

Attached is the Guildhall Clock Museum with over 700 timepieces, spanning 500 years, including a silver skull watch reputed to have belonged to Mary, Queen of Scots. On the east side of Guildhall Yard, the Guildhall Art

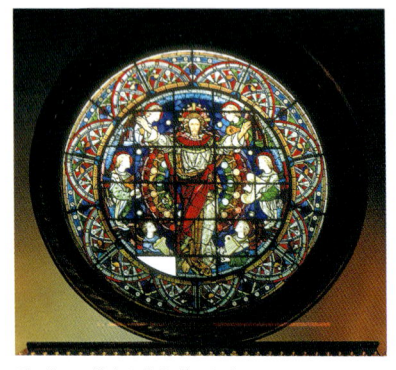

The beautiful Guildhall window

MILITARY MUSEUMS

Guards Museum
See p27.

National Army Museum
Recounts the history of the British soldier from the Battle of Agincourt (1415) to the present day.
Royal Hospital Road, SW3. Tel: (020) 7730 0717; www.national-army-museum.ac.uk. Open: daily 10am–5.30pm. Closed: 24–26 Dec, 1 Jan, Good Friday & first May Bank Holiday. Free admission. Tube: Sloane Square.

Royal Air Force Museum
A collection of over 200 aircraft along with bombs, guns and missiles, plus the story of flight.
Grahame Park Way, NW9. Tel: (020) 8205 2266 for recorded info; www.rafmuseum.org.uk. Open: daily 10am–6pm. Admission charge. Tube: Colindale.

Royal Artillery Museum
The story of guns from the 14th century to the present day.
Royal Arsenal, Woolwich, SE18. Tel: (020) 8855 7755; www.firepower.org.uk. Open: daily 10.30am–5pm. Admission charge. Rail to Woolwich Arsenal.

Gallery, replacing the gallery destroyed in the Blitz, opened in 1997.
Gresham St, EC2. Tel: (020) 7606 3030. Open: Mon–Sat 9.30am–4.45pm. Free admission. Tube: Bank.

Harrods

Once a favourite shopping venue of the Royal Family, this is still considered among the really classy department stores and is a tourist attraction in itself, especially the Food Hall. Seen at night, the exterior is ablaze with white lights.

87–135 Brompton Rd, Knightsbridge, SW1. Tel: (020) 7730 1234. www.harrods.com. Open: Mon–Sat 10am–8pm, Sun noon–6pm. Tube: Knightsbridge.

Highgate Cemetery

Elaborate tombs, symbolic empty chairs and sorrowing angels epitomise the Victorian view of death. In the original west section (seen only on tours) are the Egyptian Avenue and the Terrace Catacombs. The most visited grave of all is that of Karl Marx, appropriately in the east section!

Swain's Lane, N6. Tel: (020) 8340 1834. www.highgate-cemetery.org. East: Open: daily 10am–5pm (11am weekends, 4pm winter). West: Tours on weekdays (except Dec–Feb), at 2pm; weekends, hourly 11am–4pm (3pm winter). Admission charge. Tube: Archway.

Imperial War Museum

If you know what a Sopwith Camel is, and why Douglas Bader was so special, this is the place for you. The main 23m- (75ft-) high gallery shows a World War II V2 rocket, a Battle of Britain Spitfire, and a modern Polaris missile. 'Experiences' recall both world wars, with recreated smells and sounds of warfare. There is an air-raid shelter used during the Blitz, and a simulated Mosquito fighterbomber's night-raid over northern France. This excellent museum is an education in modern warfare.

Lambeth Rd, SE1.
Tel: (020) 7416 5320.
www.iwm.org.uk. Open: daily 10am–6pm. Closed: 24–26 Dec.
Free admission. Tube: Lambeth North or Elephant & Castle.

The magnificence of Harrods, the store that really does sell everything

Lesser-known London

Why go where everyone else goes? London is peppered with small museums that are never crowded, of which the following are a small selection. Some open only in the summer. Lesser-known London includes museums of special interest . . . to tempt doctors, dentists and garden enthusiasts . . . and more! Almost all are free. Every year, in September for one weekend only, London's public and private buildings open their doors to the public. Further information from Open House, www.openhouse.org.uk

British Dental Association Museum

Enough to put your teeth on edge! Refurbished in 2005.
64 Wimpole St, W1. Tel: (020) 7935 0875. Open: Tue & Thur 1pm–4pm (by appointment). Free admission. Tube: Bond St or Regent's Park.

Fenton House

The walled garden of this elegant red-brick William and Mary house (1693) is bliss on a fine summer's day. Inside are antique furniture, porcelain and a collection of keyboard instruments.
Hampstead Grove, NW3. Information line: (01494) 755563. www.national trust.org.uk. Open: Apr–Oct Wed–Fri 2–5pm, weekends 11am–5pm; Mar 2–5pm weekends. Admission charge. Tube: Hampstead.

Florence Nightingale Museum

'The Lady with the Lamp' was the nursing heroine of the Crimean War. Next door is St Thomas's Hospital where the Nightingale Training School launched modern nursing in the 1870s.
Gassiot House, 2 Lambeth Palace Rd, SE1. Tel: (020) 7620 0374. www.florence-nightingale.co.uk. Open: daily 10am–5pm. Closed: Good Friday–Easter Sunday & 22 Dec–2 Jan. Admission charge. Tube: Waterloo or Westminster.

Freemasons' Hall

Guided tours (must be pre-booked) explain regalia and history.

The famous couch in Sigmund Freud's study

60 Great Queen St, WC2.
Tel: (020) 7831 9811. www.ugle.org.uk.
Open: Mon–Fri 10am–5pm.
Free admission. Tube: Holborn or Covent Garden.

Freud Museum

Yes, the couch, complete with oriental rug, is in the study. Eighty-two-year-old Sigmund Freud, the father of psychoanalysis, and his daughter Anna fled here from Vienna in 1938. His books still line the shelves. There are lectures, archive films and a shop.
20 Maresfield Gardens, NW3.
Tel: (020) 7435 2002.
www.freud.org.uk.
Open: Wed–Sun noon–5pm. Admission charge. Tube: Finchley Rd.

The Garden Museum

A tribute to the Tradescant family, gardeners royal and botanists, the museum is housed in a restored church. Outside is a 17th-century-style garden.
St Mary-at-Lambeth, Lambeth Palace Rd, SE1. Tel: (020) 7401 8865. www.museumgardenhistory.org. Open: Tue–Sun 10.30am–5pm. Admission charge. Tube: Lambeth North or Westminster.

Jewish Museum

Jewish life, history, religion and art, particularly in Britain.
Raymond Burton House, 129–131 Albert St, NW1. Tel: (020) 7284 1997. www.jewishmuseum.org.uk. Reopening Autumn 2009. Contact for opening hours. Admission charge.
Tube: Camden Town.

Lesser-known London

The two Regency houses occupied by Keats and Fanny Brawne have been made into one, and are furnished in period style

Dr Johnson's House

'Lexicographer. A writer of dictionaries, a harmless drudge.' Samuel Johnson infused the first definitive *Dictionary of the English Language* (1755) with his knowledge and wit. Six assistants worked with him in the Queen Anne house, squeezed into a square off Fleet Street, where he wrote the book.
17 Gough Square, Fleet St, EC4.
Tel: (020) 7353 3745.
www.drjohnsonshouse.org.
Open: Mon–Sat 11am–5.30pm (5pm winter). Admission charge.
Tube: Chancery Lane or Temple.

Keats House and Museum

A new plum tree stands where Keats wrote his *Ode to a Nightingale*. His house, crammed with mementoes, is next door to that of his fiancée, Fanny Brawne. Keats died aged 25 in 1821 before they could be married.
10 Keats Grove, NW3.
Tel: (020) 7435 2062. Reopening summer 2009. Contact for opening hours.
Admission charge. Tube: Hampstead.

Kensington Palace

This was home to Diana, Princess of Wales, and other members of the Royal Family who have followed the choice of King William III (he left the damp of Whitehall Palace for this area). Christopher Wren and his assistant Nicholas Hawksmoor redesigned the house, but it owes much of its present appearance to William Kent and James Wyatt. Monarchs were born, lived and died here until Queen Victoria left her birthplace for Buckingham Palace. The room where this shy 18-year-old was told she was Britain's new Queen on 20 June 1837 is one of the State Apartments on show. Another highlight is the Royal Ceremonial Dress Collection, displaying

The original Victorian operating theatre at St Thomas' Hospital

Nearby attractions
Military museums (*see pp27, 60 & 61*).
Sporting museums (*see p160 & p161*).
Museums for children (*see pp152–3*).
Steam Museum and Musical Museum (*see p123*).

dresses and uniforms worn at court. *Kensington Gardens, W8. Tel: 0844 482 7777. www.hrp.org.uk. Open: daily 10am–6pm. Admission charge. Tube: High St Kensington or Queensway.*

Kenwood House (The Iveagh Bequest)
Rembrandt's *Self-Portrait* is the most famous of many important works of art to feature in the Iveagh Bequest, set in this elegant villa remodelled by Robert Adam high above Hampstead. Visitors can also see great paintings by Turner, Gainsborough, Reynolds, Vermeer and Frans Hals. An effort to reach, but well worth it, especially in summer for the open-air classical music concerts. *Hampstead Lane, NW3. Tel: (020) 8348 1286. www.english-heritage.org.uk. Open: daily 11.30am–4pm. Closed: 24–26 Dec & 1 Jan. Free admission. Tube: Hampstead or Golders Green, and then bus 210.*

Lambeth Palace
Although the official home of the Archbishop of Canterbury since the early 13th century, the gatehouse is a red-brick Tudor masterpiece. *Lambeth Palace Rd, SE1. Tel: (020) 7898 1200. www.archbishopofcanterbury.org.*

Tours by request Feb–Nov (limited numbers). Tube: Westminster or Lambeth North.

Leighton House Museum
Lord Leighton, the Victorian painter and art collector, built this house as a private art gallery. This museum will reopen at the end of 2009.
12 Holland Park Rd, W14.
Tel: (020) 7602 3316. Open: Wed–Mon 11am–5.30pm. Admission charge. Tube: Kensington High St. Buses: 9, 10, 27 or 49 to Odeon Cinema.

Lincoln's Inn
The most attractive of the four Inns of Court, built in 1490, and restored early in the 20th century. Dickens' *Bleak House* opens in the Old Hall. A host of prime ministers studied law here – as

The Foundling Museum has some rococo interiors from the original 1741 hospital

Lesser-known London

65

Lloyd's of London – modernist architecture

did Oliver Cromwell. (*See also* Legal London Walk, *pp68–9*.)
Lincoln's Inn, WC2. Tel: (020) 7405 1393. www.lincolnsinn.org.uk.
Grounds open: Mon–Fri 7am–7pm. Free admission. Tube: Holborn, Temple or Chancery Lane.

Lloyd's of London

Insurance has come a long way, from Edward Lloyd's 17th-century coffee house to Richard Rogers' 1986 'inside-out' building. Lloyd's of London is a society of underwriters who accept risks on giant ocean-going tankers, as well as the legs of famous ballet dancers. The building is not open to the public.
1 Lime St, EC3. Tube: Bank, Monument or Liverpool St.

The London Dungeon

Candles flicker, water drips, a figure on the rack groans in agony: this is the museum of medieval horror. Not advised for very young children, nor for squeamish adults.
Tooley St, SE1. www.thedungeons.com.
Open: daily 10.30am–5.30pm.
Admission charge.
Tube: London Bridge.

MCC Museum

The world's oldest sports museum is at Lord's cricket ground, with a priceless collection of cricketing memorabilia, dating from 1864 and still growing. There is a cinema screening early films of cricket. The visit is included in the tour of Lord's cricket ground.
St John's Wood Rd, NW8. Tel: (020) 7616 8595. www.lords.org.
Open: 10am, noon & 2pm. Admission charge. Tube: Baker Street, St John's Wood, Warwick Avenue.

Museum of the Order of St John

The history of the order, stretching from the ancient warrior monks of the Crusades through to the modern St John Ambulance Brigade.
St John's Gate, St John's Lane, EC1.
Tel: (020) 7324 4005. www.sja.org.uk.
Open: Mon–Fri 10am–5pm, Sat 10am–4pm. Closed: all Bank Holiday weekends. Free admission.
Tube: Farringdon.

Old Operating Theatre Museum

Victorian operating theatre with suitably gruesome displays.
9A St Thomas Street, SE1.
Tel: (020) 7188 2679.

*www.thegarret.org.uk.
Open: daily 10.30am–5pm.
Closed: 15 Dec–5 Jan. Admission charge.
Tube: London Bridge.*

Spencer House

London's finest surviving 18th-century town house was built by the first Earl Spencer, an ancestor of Diana, Princess of Wales, and restored at a cost of £16 million.
27 St James's Place, SW1. Tel: (020) 7499 8620. www.spencerhouse.co.uk. Open: Sun 10.30am–5.45pm (except Jan & Aug). Admission charge. Tube: Green Park.

Thomas Coram Foundation (Foundling Museum)

A copy of Handel's score of The Messiah is just one of the treasures in this former hospital for abandoned children.
40 Brunswick Square, WC1. Tel: (020) 7841 3600. www.foundlingmuseum.org.uk. Open: Tue–Sat 10am–5pm, Sun 11am–5pm. Admission charge. Tube: Russell Square.

Wallace Collection

Frans Hals's *Laughing Cavalier* and Fragonard's *The Swing* are two of the stars of a superb collection of European art in this intimate and interesting museum.
Hertford House, Manchester Square, W1. Tel: (020) 7563 9500. www.wallacecollection.org. Open: daily 10am–5pm. Free admission. Tube: Bond St or Marble Arch.

Scare yourself silly at the London Dungeon

Walk: Legal London

This walk goes through the Inns of Court, the ancient enclaves of lawyers, and takes in some of the traditions associated with the law.

Allow 1 hour.

Start at Temple underground station. Turn left along Victoria Embankment and left into Middle Temple Lane (access Monday to Friday 9am–5pm).

1 The Inns of Court
In these medieval colleges of the law, the most powerful lawyers in the land work. Traffic-free courtyards and some of London's last surviving gas lamps add to yesteryear's atmosphere.
Go up the hill; on the left is Middle Temple Hall.

2 Middle Temple Hall
This hall was opened by Elizabeth I in 1576 and is still a functioning dining room. It is open to visitors 10am–noon Monday to Friday except when functions are organised. Shakespeare's *Twelfth Night* was first performed here in February 1602.
Go uphill on Middle Temple Lane; a few metres on the right is Pump Court Cloisters. Proceed to the second courtyard. This is the Inner Temple, whose symbol is Pegasus, the winged horse seen on the wall opposite Temple Church.

3 Temple Church
This is one of the few Norman round churches left in England, the shape supposedly inspired by the Holy Sepulchre Church in Jerusalem (*Open: Mon–Fri 10am–4pm*).
Retrace your footsteps. Turn right on Middle Temple Lane and continue up to Fleet St. Turn right.

4 Fleet Street
Fleet Street was synonymous with printing presses for 500 years, until new technology took the newspapers elsewhere. Opposite on the far right is the church of St Dunstan-in-the-West, where Betsy Trotwood and David Copperfield admired Gog and Magog striking the quarter hours on the clock outside, in Charles Dickens' famous novel. Did they also notice the statue of Elizabeth I set in the wall below it? John Donne, the famous poet and

Dean of St Paul's Cathedral, was rector here from 1624 to 1631, and is commemorated by a monument inside the church. A lot of publications at that time were published in the churchyard. Today, Eastern Orthodox services are held here by the Romanian community.

5 Taverns and tea

Opposite the church, Ye Olde Cock Tavern claims to be the oldest hostelry in Fleet Street, and almost hidden up a narrow staircase at No 17 are **Prince Henry's Rooms**, with a decorated ceiling dating from 1610 (*Open: Mon–Fri 11am–2pm*). Diagonally opposite Wren's flamboyant entrance to Middle Temple Lane, the defiant, pedestalled Griffin, unofficial badge of the City, guards the entrance to the City of London. Originally, this was the site of the Old Temple Bar gateway. Since 1706, Twining's have been selling tea and coffee in the 'narrowest shop in London', No 216.

Cross at the pedestrian crossing for the Law Courts.

6 The Law Courts

Officially the Royal Courts of Justice, the 100-year-old Victorian Gothic building has over 1,000 rooms dealing with civil (non-criminal) as well as criminal appeal cases.

Walk along Fleet St to Chancery Lane and turn left.

7 Chancery Lane

At No 93, Ede and Ravenscroft still make the wigs and robes for judges and barristers. The bomb-proof basement stores royal robes of state.

Turn back and enter Carey St.

8 Lincoln's Inn Fields

The Tudor and neo-Tudor brick buildings of Lincoln's Inn have a record of 11 prime ministers as students, from Walpole to Margaret Thatcher. It has the finest gardens of any of the 14th-century Inns of Court. Continuing anti-clockwise around the Fields, Nos 12–13 contain one of London's most intriguing museums, the eclectic collection of 19th-century architect Sir John Soane (*Open: Mon–Fri 10am–4pm only*).

Exit Lincoln's Inn Fields on Gate St which leads to Holborn underground station.

London Silver Vaults

Buried in real vaults two storeys under ground, this is a 100-year-old Aladdin's cave of antique and new silver that is for sale. The vaults display the wares of 37 shops, where you can get specialist advice and buy at dealers' prices.
Chancery House, Chancery Lane, WC2. Tel: (020) 7242 3844.
www.thesilvervaults.com.
Open: Mon–Fri 9am–5.30pm, Sat 9am–1pm. Free admission.
Tube: Chancery Lane.

London Transport Museum

The underground system is over 140 years old. Before its existence, there were horse-drawn buses, trams and a steam-powered underground railway. See them on display in the former Flower Market of Covent Garden, which is decorated with London Transport posters.
39 Wellington St, Covent Garden Piazza, WC2. Tel: (020) 7379 6344.
www.ltmuseum.co.uk. Open: Sat–Thur 10am–6pm, Fri 11am–9pm.
Admission charge. Tube: Covent Garden.

London Zoo

One of the world's oldest zoos. You may encounter some of the 15,000 animals at close quarters in a daily programme of events, including keeper talks.
Regent's Park, NW1.
Tel: (020) 7722 3333. www.zsl.org.
Open: daily 10am–5.30pm, winter 4pm.
Admission charge.
Tube: Camden Town.

Madame Tussauds

Pavarotti, Humphrey Bogart, Marilyn Monroe and the Beckhams are all here – in wax, of course. More gruesome figures lurk in the Chamber of Horrors. The oldest figure dates back to 1765, and a studio shows how they are made. Next door is the building that used to house the London Planetarium, but which Madame Tussauds has turned into the Auditorium. It presents a show based on celebrities, created by the team behind Wallace and Gromit, of *Chicken Run* fame.
Marylebone Rd, NW1. Tel: 0870 999 0046.
www.madametussauds.com.
Open: daily 9.30am–5.30pm.
Tube: Baker St.

The Mall

This pink asphalt, tree-lined boulevard runs from Trafalgar Square to Buckingham Palace, and can be seen at

THE GREAT FIRE

A staggering 176 hectares (430 acres) in and around the City of London were destroyed by the fire of 1666. Houses, tightly packed and built mainly of wood, were pulled down with firehooks, doused with water from 'squirts' (like oversized water-pistols) or even blown up to try to slow the fire. A drought had left a water shortage, and wind swept the flames through 400 streets from the river to the modern Barbican, and from the Tower of London to the Inner Temple. After five days, the fire was stopped, having destroyed 13,200 homes, 89 churches, plus the Guildhall, St Paul's Cathedral and the Royal Exchange. It had all started in a bakery in Pudding Lane (*see* The Monument, *opposite*).

its best on state occasions when the Queen travels to and from the palace. *Closed to traffic on Sun and public holidays. Tube: Victoria, Trafalgar Square or Green Park.*

Mansion House

The Lord Mayor of London's official residence. The Egyptian Hall, with 16 Corinthian columns, barrel-vaulted ceiling and stained-glass windows, is not open to the general public, and is seen only by a privileged few – often at banquets when the Lord Mayor sits on the throne-like Chair of State.
Mansion House St, EC4. www.cityoflondon.gov.uk. Open: apply to Principal Assistant (tours booked a year in advance). Free admission. Tube: Bank.

The Monument

This simple column designed by Christopher Wren commemorates the Great Fire of London, and stands 62m (203ft) tall, the exact distance to the bakery in Pudding Lane where the fire began on 2 September 1666. A total of 311 steps rise up a steeply spiral staircase to a viewing platform. There is no lift. Due to the number of tall buildings that have sprouted around it, a movement began in early 2005 to transfer the Monument closer to the Thames, although it hasn't moved yet!
Monument St, EC3.
Tel: (020) 7626 2717. Open: daily 10am–5.30pm. Admission charge. Tube: Monument.

Vehicles galore at the London Transport Museum

Monuments, statues and sculptures

Monuments and statues reflect the history of England, but there are also sculptures and delightful whimsical pieces by well-known artists. The following are just a few.

Monuments

Eleanor Cross

Eleanor was the beloved Queen of Edward I. She died in Nottinghamshire in 1290, and each stop of the funeral procession back to London was marked with a cross. This is a replica of the final one before her entombment in Westminster Abbey.
Charing Cross station forecourt.
Tube: Charing Cross or Embankment.

Marble Arch

Designed by Nash in 1827 as a triumphal gateway for George IV's redesigned Buckingham Palace, Marble Arch was moved here by Queen Victoria when it was discovered to be too narrow to accommodate the passage of the State Coaches. On the tiny traffic island opposite, a small brass plaque marks the site of the infamous Tyburn Gallows, where prisoners were hanged in public.
Marble Arch, W1.
Tube: Marble Arch.

Statues

The South Bank Lion

Designed by WF Woodington, this is the largest of several sculptures in London made out of Coade stone, a tough artificial stone.
Westminster Bridge, SE1.
Tube: Westminster.

James II

A bronze statue attributed to Grinling Gibbons, this tubby 'Jacobus Secundus', dressed like a Roman general, dates

---

OUT OF SIGHT

To see some wonderful sculptures, look up – above doorways, on walls, even on top of buildings. George I stands on top of the steeple of St George's Church, Bloomsbury. A bust of Shakespeare leans out, as if from a window in the Shakespeare's Head pub, on the corner of Foubert's Place and Carnaby Street. London's oldest outdoor statue dates from 1320 BC; the Egyptian lion-headed goddess Sekhmet over the doorway of Sotheby's, the famous auctioneers, at 34–35 New Bond Street.

from 1686, and is usually regarded as the finest statue in London.
In front of the National Gallery, Trafalgar Square, WC2. Tube: Leicester Square or Charing Cross.

Peter Pan
Since 1912 Peter has stood playing his pipes on a bronze rock in Kensington Gardens, his home before Neverland. His creator, JM Barrie, lived nearby and wrote the stories for three boys he met in this park.
Kensington Gardens, W2. Tube: Lancaster Gate.

Queen Boadicea
This ancient British Queen of the Iceni tribe looks as if she is rallying her troops to take on the Romans. Having dealt them a massive defeat in AD 61, her troops were similarly routed later in the year. She preferred poison to capture.
Westminster Bridge, SW1. Tube: Westminster.

Sculpture
Horse and Rider by Elizabeth Frink
Since 1975, this unassuming bronze statue of a young man on a horse takes pedestrians by surprise.
Corner of Dover St and Piccadilly. Tube: Green Park.

Boy on a Dolphin by David Wynne
A delightful bronze, full of movement. The little boy flies through the air, his left hand holding on to the dorsal fin of the leaping dolphin.
Pier House, Oakley St at Albert Bridge, SW3. Tube: Sloane Square, then bus 22, 19 or 49 to Oakley St.

Guardian of the South Bank

Museum of London

The story of the city and its people, from 400,000 BC to the 21st century, is told through paintings, photographs, ornaments, furniture and clothing. History comes to life, dates make sense and the visitor will get much more out of the rest of the trip to the capital.

London before London 400,000 BC–AD 50

See how the Thames Valley was affected by the ice ages and the first people to live in what is now London. Take a look at a flint hand-axe and bronze spearheads and see how tools and weapons were developed.

Children looking at Viking weapons in the Medieval Gallery

Roman London AD 43–410

Excavations for office blocks often uncover Roman remains. From the site at 90 Queen Street, counters for games, iron knives, and bone and jet hairpins were found. Part of the Roman Wall, once 6m (20ft) high, and encircling 134 hectares (331 acres) of the City, is also here (there are several sections around the City). The ruins of a Roman temple stand on Queen Victoria Street.

Medieval London

See what London Bridge looked like, with 20 arches topped by a row of buildings; and St Paul's Cathedral, used as offices by lawyers in between services.

London's Burning (until winter 2009)

This is a free exhibition exploring how the Great Fire shaped the London we know today. Fewer than a dozen people died but within five days of the fire starting in Pudding Lane in September 1666 it had destroyed four-fifths of the City of London. Discover the story of the fire through real-life experiences, some famous and some lesser known, using interactive, video and conventional displays.

Redevelopment

The Museum of London will be undergoing major changes until early 2010. The £18 million redevelopment will transform how it tells the story of London from 1666 to the present day – incorporating more diverse histories and 25 per cent more gallery space. Throughout the redevelopment visitors will still be able to enjoy the Museum's prehistoric, Roman and Medieval London galleries and an exciting range of events for all ages.

Museum of London. 150 London Wall, EC2. Tel: 020 7001 9844.
www.museumoflondon.org.uk.
Open: daily 10am–6pm. Free admission.
Tube: Barbican, St Paul's, Moorgate.

An artist's impression of the Great Fire of London

Museum in Docklands

This museum is ideally placed to let you explore the 2,000-year history of the river, port and people of this part of London. From the Roman and Saxon port through to the office blocks of Canary Wharf today, there are four floors of interactive displays, archaeological finds, objects, paintings, reconstructions, and historical photographs and documents. There is also a restaurant and bar called 1802 which is open for food during the day and for drinks in the evening.

The museum was originally a sugar warehouse. It is one of the most significant surviving buildings in Britain and was integral to the slave trade. In October 2007 it opened London's first dedicated slave-trade gallery, looking at the role London and Londoners played in the transatlantic slave trade and the legacy this heritage has left in the capital.

Other galleries include:

Museum in Docklands is housed in an old sugar warehouse

A reconstruction of the Sailortown quarter

Thames Highway AD 50–1600

As far back as AD 61 London was described as an 'important centre for merchants' with goods arriving from across the Roman Empire – often in the amphora on display here. Follow the story of how the port grew throughout the medieval period.

The Coming of the Docks 1800–20

Port facilities were failing to keep up with growth in trade, but by 1810, after the West India Docks, London Docks and East India Docks had opened, London had the best port facilities in the world. Paintings and artefacts illustrate what it was like on the bustling waterfront.

Sailortown 1840–50

A recreation of the maze of streets, lanes and alleyways lets you experience for yourself the sights, sounds and smells of life for the people who lived in the area behind the wharves and docks, with its reputation for pimps, prostitutes and smugglers.

Docklands at War 1939–45

As well as bearing the brunt of enemy attack during the World War II the port and its communities played a vital part in Britain's fight-back. Archive film footage shows the terrible loss of lives and goods, and interactive screens let you listen to local people's wartime memories.

West India Quay, Canary Wharf, E14.
Tel: 020 7001 9844.
www.museumindocklands.org.uk.
Open: daily 10am-6pm.
Admission charge for over-16s.
Tube: Canary Wharf.
DLR: West India Quay.

Museum in Docklands

National Gallery

One of the world's great permanent collections of paintings, the venerable National Gallery was given a new injection of life in 1991 with the opening of the Sainsbury Wing for the Early Renaissance Collection. Five new floors provide space for the new policy of hanging paintings chronologically rather than geographically.

A mere 38 pictures started the National Collection in 1824, but these included Rubens's *Rape of the Sabine Women*, Titian's *Venus and Adonis* and Rembrandt's *Adoration of the Shepherds*. Subsequent additions mean that great artists like Velázquez, Van Dyck and Holbein are arguably better represented here than in their home countries.

Sainsbury Wing

This special setting and controlled environment is ideal for the oldest and most fragile works. Grey plaster walls enhance the vibrant colours and gilding of pictures, many of which were painted originally for churches.

The Battle of San Romano by Paolo Uccello (room 55) is an important landmark in art, showing the (then) new theory of perspective. Flemish painters were experimenting, too, with light as well as perspective, as Jan Van Eyck's *The Arnolfini Portrait* shows in the next room (56). Some experts think the man in the mirror is Van Eyck himself.

Room 51 has a lively sketch of the *Virgin and Child with St John the Baptist and St Anne* by Leonardo da Vinci. A version of Leonardo's *Virgin of the Rocks* is nearby.

West Wing

Technical advances in the early 16th century were rapid as European painters learnt from one another. Hans Holbein the Younger painted *The Ambassadors* (room 4) in 1533. What is remarkable is the trick of perspective he plays on the viewer – stand at the right-hand side of the picture to decipher the elongated white object in the foreground. The correct angle will reveal a skull.

North Wing

In the 17th century, courts competed for the services of the best painters. Rubens worked in Italy, Spain and England, but the woman in *The Straw Hat* (room 22) is probably his sister-in-law, not a noblewoman.

Sir Anthony Van Dyck made his name as painter to Charles I. His *Equestrian Portrait of Charles I* (room 30) is vast and imposing.

Next door in room 29 is the *Rokeby Venus*, a Velázquez painting that shocked 17th-century Spain because of the naked flesh it depicted.

Five rooms away is Rembrandt's moving *Self-Portrait aged 63*, painted just before he died in 1669. Sixty self-portraits by the great Dutch artist survive (room 27).

East Wing

Although the bulk of Turner's paintings are at the Tate Britain, eight of his finest are here, including *The Fighting Téméraire* (room 34). In the same room, John Constable's *The Hay Wain* captures the constantly changing light of East Anglia.

Nearby are two contrasting works. Ingres's *Madame Moitessier* (room 41) took 12 years and three changes of design (and dress!) before she was ready to face the world. Claude Monet's sketch of *Bathers at La Grenouillère* (room 43) was completed rapidly, using bold brush strokes in what is a forerunner to Impressionism.

The National Gallery, Trafalgar Square, WC2. Tel: (020) 7747 2885.
www.nationalgallery.org.uk.
Open: daily 10am–6pm, Wed until 9pm.
Free admission; charge for special temporary exhibitions.
Free guided tours and lectures.
Tube: Charing Cross or Leicester Square.

Nearby attractions
National Portrait Gallery (*see p80*).
Trafalgar Square (*see p114*).

The National Gallery building of 1824, overlooking the fountains of Trafalgar Square

National Portrait Gallery

Famous British people throughout the centuries are presented in paintings, sculptures, drawings, cartoons, miniatures, silhouettes and photographs. Does Richard III really look like a child-killer? Compare a sorrowful Charles I with a stern Oliver Cromwell. Try and work out why a 17th-century country girl, Nell Gwyn, fascinated the shrewd, lascivious Charles II.

The Victorian founders hoped this gallery would be an incentive 'to mental exertion, to noble actions, to good conduct'. Nowadays, we admit to nosiness about celebrities. Art lovers appreciate works by Hogarth, Joshua Reynolds and Thomas Lawrence; students of fashion examine details of the clothes. Start at the top with the Tudors and descend chronologically, wander at will or head straight for your favourite famous person.
St Martin's Place, WC2. Tel: 020 7306 0055. www.npg.org.uk. Open: daily 10am–6pm, Thur & Fri until 9pm. Free admission, except for special exhibitions. Tube: Leicester Square or Charing Cross.

Natural History Museum

'First of all it looks like a cathedral, then inside it has everything you want to know about life and the earth,' is one nine-year-old's verdict. Since its 1881 opening, millions have enjoyed this buff-and-blue terracotta museum, decorated with sculptures of fish, lizards, monkeys, even bats! The 26m- (85ft-) long Diplodocus skeleton waits just inside the entrance. First are the Life Galleries, then the Earth Galleries, which incorporate the former Geological Museum.

Hands-on fun

Push down on a springed 'horse's leg' and compare it with an 'elephant's leg' or hear a mother's heartbeat as a baby would inside the womb. The high-tech tricks of computers, videos and quiz

The stately façade of the Natural History Museum

games are balanced by old-fashioned rooms with specimens under glass. There are 11 main exhibitions, but many regulars are tempted back by new attractions.

Ecology rules OK!
Opened in 1991, the Ecology Gallery illustrates the delicate balance in our environment. Step inside a leaf to discover how photosynthesis works, watch the reproduction cycle of a rabbit or hear the history of a coral reef.

Here's to the Creepy-Crawlies
Dedicated to arthropods, the Creepy-Crawly Gallery has the low-down on spiders, crustaceans and insects. Did you know that spiders have hair? Children love No 1 Crawley House, where humans are out, but flies, lice and fleas are in!

Earth Galleries
The simulation of the earthquake in Kobe is a highlight, but there is also a fabulous collection of gems, including diamonds from Siberia and Africa.
Cromwell Rd, SW7. Tel: (020) 7942 5000. www.nhm.ac.uk. Open: daily 10am–5.50pm. Free admission; charge for special exhibitions.
Tube: South Kensington.

Old Bailey
Officially called the Central Criminal Court, but nicknamed after the street, this is the scene of lurid trials, from Oscar Wilde's homosexual revelations

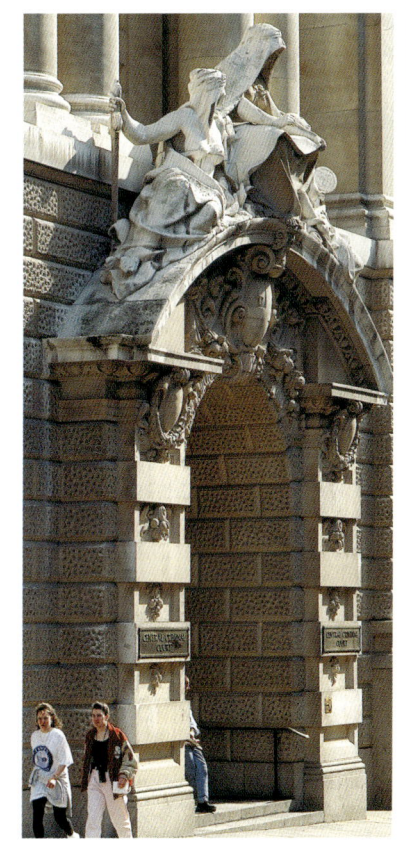

The Central Criminal Court or Old Bailey

to the 'Yorkshire Ripper' murder case. It is open to the public, but expect queues for the newsworthy trials. Once the site of Newgate Prison with gallows just outside, its last public hanging was in 1868. Note that the gilded statue of Justice on the top is not blindfolded.
Old Bailey, EC4. Tel: (020) 7248 3277. Open: Mon–Fri 10am–1pm, & 2–4pm when court is sitting. Free admission.
Tube: St Paul's.

Pall Mall

Pall Mall is a broad 19th-century street lined with large houses, including many exclusive gentlemen's clubs. The strange name comes from *paille-maille*, a croquet-like game played by aristocrats in the 17th century. Gas street lighting began here in 1807.
Pall Mall, SW1. Tube: Green Park or Piccadilly Circus.

Piccadilly Circus

A meeting place since it was built in 1819 to connect Regent Street with Piccadilly, and once regarded as the centre of the Empire, Piccadilly Circus is full of contrasts. Handsome buildings are covered in neon advertisements, and traffic roars past Eros, the first-ever statue cast in aluminium. An Angel of Christian Charity rather than Cupid, it was a tribute to the philanthropic Earl of Shaftesbury, a supporter of reforms in factories and other workplaces, and of child welfare.
Piccadilly Circus, W1.
Tube: Piccadilly Circus.

Regent Street

A sweeping curve joining Piccadilly Circus and Oxford Circus, this is one of London's most exclusive shopping streets. Well-known names range from Aquascutum and Hamleys, the toy shop, to Liberty. This is the backbone of John Nash's elegant early 1800s plan for central London.
Tube: Piccadilly Circus or Oxford Circus.

CHRISTMAS LIGHTS

From early November, the Christmas lights are switched on nightly in Regent Street and Oxford Street, Knightsbridge and Brompton Road. Londoners also enjoy the decorations in smaller shopping streets such as Bond and Jermyn Streets, Beauchamp Place and Covent Garden. These tend to be less showy and more traditional. As for stores, Selfridges on Oxford Street and Hamleys on Regent Street always create special window scenes, while those of Harvey Nichols in Knightsbridge are perhaps the most stylish in town. Harrods looks like a huge Christmas ornament all year round.

Royal Academy of Arts

This is the oldest fine arts institution in the country, founded in 1768 by George III. A statue of Sir Joshua Reynolds, its first president, stands in the courtyard of the impressive mansion Burlington House. The Academy holds annual exhibitions ranging from the 240-year-old Summer Exhibition of living artists to temporary exhibitions, often from other countries. The permanent art collection includes a marble sculpture, *Virgin and Child with the Infant St John*, by Michelangelo. The Sackler Galleries provide additional hanging space and opened-up views into the garden.

Piccadilly, W1.
Tel: (020) 7300 8000.
www.royalacademy.org.uk.
Open: daily during exhibitions,
10am–6pm, Fri until 10pm. Admission
charge for exhibitions. Tube: Green Park
or Piccadilly Circus.

Royal Courts of Justice

Often called simply the Law Courts, this neo-Gothic combination of arches and turrets hears civil cases, such as divorces and bankruptcy, as well as criminal appeals. Visitors can watch from the Public Galleries in 60 courts.
The Strand, WC2.
Tel: (020) 7947 6000. Open: Courts
(when in session) 10.30am–1pm &
2–4.30pm; building 9.30am–4.30pm.
Free admission. Tube: Temple.

Royal Hospital, Chelsea

About 400 scarlet-coated army pensioners live in Sir Christopher Wren's grand riverside retirement home. Founded by Charles II for army veterans, the pensioners now wear a modernised version of the Duke of Marlborough's army uniform (early 1700s) and tricorne hats.

The heart of Chelsea Hospital is the chapel with its battle flags, and the Great Hall overlooking Figure Court with its statue of Charles II. On Oak Apple Day (29 May) the pensioners used to get double rations to celebrate their founder's birthday and decorate the statue with oak leaves – a reminder of how the king escaped the Parliamentarians by hiding in an oak tree after the Battle of Worcester (1651). These days they parade on Founder's Day (early June; not open to the public). The 11am Parade Service in the chapel on Sundays is a grand sight – as is the annual Chelsea Flower Show held in late May in the gardens (which are open to the public throughout the year, except Christmas Day, Founder's Day and some days prior to the Flower Show).
Royal Hospital Rd, SW3. Tel: (020) 7881
5200. www.chelsea-pensioners.org.uk.
Open: daily 10am–noon & 2–4pm.
Closed: Oct–Mar Sun and all Bank
Holidays. Free admission. Tube:
Sloane Square.

The heart of London, Piccadilly Circus

Walk: Gentlemen's London

The area enclosed by Piccadilly, Lower Regent Street, Pall Mall and St James's has always been select, full of fine shops, squares and exclusive gentlemen's clubs.

Allow 1 hour.

Start at Piccadilly Circus underground station. Exit via subway 3, Piccadilly (south side). Go downhill on Regent St and turn right on to Jermyn St.

1 Jermyn Street
In the early 19th century, tailors and shirtmakers set up shop to cater for the needs of gentlemen in nearby clubs, while jewellers and perfumers provided for wives and mistresses. Shops still have a Regency air, with burnished brass, mahogany-framed windows and old-fashioned service. Geo. F. Trumper (No 20) were barbers to crowned heads of state; order up a club, company or military tie (or design your own!) at TM Lewin (No 106). Cheese is the speciality of Paxton & Whitfield (No 93). At Floris (No 89), perfumes and toiletries are still sold by descendants of the Spaniard who founded the shop in 1730. Shirtmakers like Hawes & Curtis (No 23), Hilditch & Key (No 73), Harvie & Hudson (No 77) and Turnbull Asser (Nos 71–72) offer stripes galore.

Turn left on to Duke St and St James's, and left again on to King St. Proceed to St James's Square; circle it clockwise.

2 Arts and clubs
Duke Street, Ryder Street and King Street abound with fine art and antique specialists, as well as Christie's, the auctioneers. St James's Square is pure

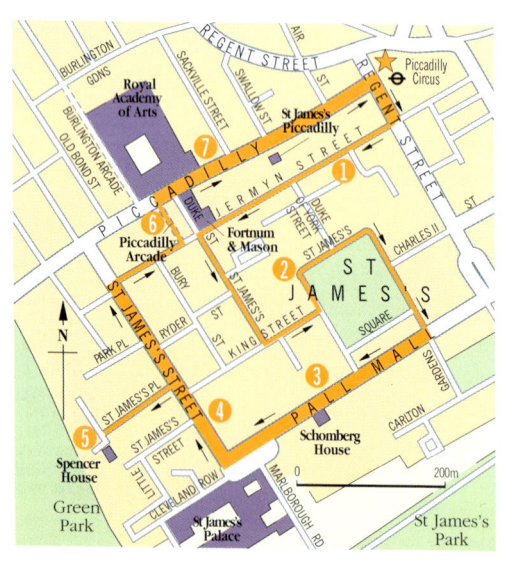

Establishment, with the East India, Devonshire and Public Schools Club (No 16), the private London Library (No 14) and the Royal Institute of International Affairs (Nos 9–10), known by its address 'Chatham House', where three prime ministers have lived. In April 1984, the killing of policewoman Yvonne Fletcher shocked the world. The shot came from No 5, the Libyan People's Bureau; her memorial is opposite. During World War II, General Eisenhower planned Operations Torch (North Africa) and Overlord (D-Day) from No 31. In the gardens of the square, William III sits astride a horse, under whose rear foot is a sculpted molehill, responsible for his fatal fall.
Leave the square by the southeastern exit and turn right on to Pall Mall.

3 Pall Mall

The painter Thomas Gainsborough lived at Schomberg House (Nos 80–82). Nell Gwyn, orange seller and courtesan, lived next door (No 79). (*See p82.*)
Turn right into St James's St.

4 St James's Street

At No 3, wine and spirit merchants Berry Bros & Rudd have been serving nobility for over 300 years, and Lock's, the hatters, at No 5 (founded 1676) designed a special hat for a Mr William Coke (made by Thomas and William Bowler) that became known as a bowler, though Lock's still call it a 'Coke'.
Turn left into St James's Place.

5 Spencer House

Looking like a period film set, St James's Place ends at the magnificently restored Spencer House. The 200-year-old London home belonging to the family of Prince Charles's late wife, Diana, is filled with art treasures.
Return to St James's St. Continue up the hill, turn right into Jermyn St, and left into Piccadilly Arcade.

6 Piccadilly Arcade

Like its northerly neighbour, Burlington Arcade, this is an early 'shopping mall'.
Turn right on to Piccadilly.

7 Piccadilly

Opposite Piccadilly Arcade is Burlington House, now the Royal Academy of Arts (*see pp82–3*). Outside Fortnum & Mason, Mr Fortnum and Mr Mason strike the hour on the big clock. Further along, Hatchards have been booksellers since 1797. Finally, visit the Church of St James's Piccadilly, which is one of Wren's finest designs.
Return to Piccadilly Circus station.

The Fortnum & Mason clock

St Paul's Cathedral

St Paul's Cathedral must be the capital's grandest building. Its 111m- (364ft-) high dome still dominates the skyline, despite the surrounding office blocks. Sir Christopher Wren's design replaced a vast Gothic cathedral destroyed in the Great Fire of 1666 (a model of which is in the cathedral's crypt). A church has been located on this site since AD 604.

Before the ruins of the Gothic edifice were cold, Wren had produced his plan – light, airy and bright compared with its gloomy predecessor. It took a mere 35 years to build the cathedral. Despite the debate over Wren's plans, we can still see much of his original ideas of 'the best Greek and Roman architecture'. The scale is monumental: 20-tonne stone blocks were shipped from Dorset on the south coast, taking two weeks to haul the final 500m (550yds) from the Thames. The scaffolding stood for over 20 years.

At the same time, Wren was supervising the rebuilding of 50 City churches. Aged 78 when St Paul's was finished, he died 13 years later. The single bell would ring out to signal the end of lunch break and still does daily at 1pm.

The nave
Looking up the nave to the high altar, arches, domes and piers present a constantly changing pattern of space.

Although Wren never intended any statues or monuments to clutter up the clean lines of his design, a huge monument to the Duke of Wellington was begun in 1852 and finally completed in 1912, 60 years after Wellington's death.

The choir and dome
It is best to sit down before looking up at the dome. The eight pictures of the life of St Paul were painted in monochrome in order to cut costs! As well as an organ once played by Handel and Mendelssohn, a choir of 54 is needed to fill the cathedral with sound. In total 18 men sing with the 36 boys who receive free education at the Choir School, rehearsing for two hours a day.

The ambulatory
A Frenchman, Jean Tijou, created the handsome gilded iron gates. One of Henry Moore's last works, *Mother and Child* (1984), is placed near the Modern Martyrs' Chapel. It commemorates,

among others, Steve Biko (who died in South Africa in 1977). Behind the high altar, where Prince Charles married Lady Diana Spencer in 1981, is the American Memorial Chapel honouring Americans who died in World War II. The high altar itself, a modern replacement for a bomb-damaged Victorian reredos, is dedicated to the Commonwealth citizens who died in the two world wars.

In the south ambulatory, the only sculpture to have survived the Great Fire intact from the old cathedral is the haunting figure of John Donne, poet and Dean of St Paul's in the early 17th century. He posed for this in a shroud *before* he died.

The crypt

Of the 350 memorials and 100 tombs down in the crypt, none matches this simple inscription to Wren:
Lector, si monumentum requiris, Circumspice – 'Reader, if you are looking for a memorial, just look around you'. A model of English understatement.

The galleries

The Whispering Gallery (259 steps up) deserves its name; face the wall, speak softly, and your words will be heard clearly on the opposite side of the gallery. Higher is the Stone Gallery with a fine view out over London. For the dizzy panorama of the Golden Gallery, be prepared for a total climb of 627 steps.
St Paul's Churchyard, EC4. Tel: (020) 7236 4128. www.stpauls.co.uk.
Cathedral open: Mon–Sat 8.30am–4pm.
Special services or events may close all or part of the cathedral.
Tours: 10.45am, 11.15am, 1.30pm, 2pm (charge). Admission charge.
Tube: St Paul's.

Magnificent St Paul's has a beautiful dome 34m (112ft) in diameter

The Science Museum

This vast walk-in encyclopedia provides the answers to millions of 'how?' and 'why?' questions. It is impossible not to find something of interest among more than 200,000 exhibits on seven floors. However, be warned: the sheer size of this museum can be overwhelming; rather than just wandering, pick up a free map and plan what you want to see, particularly if you are taking children.

The mezzanine gallery is a good place to start for an overview of the museum.

Power

'I sell here, Sir, what all the world desires to have . . . power.' When do you think that was said? 1976 about oil? 1876 about coal? No, in 1776, by Matthew Boulton, about his engine that ran on steam. Among the giant engines here that helped start the Industrial Revolution is the massive Rotative Steam Engine by Boulton and Watt which worked for 70 years.

Foucault's Pendulum

Ever wanted proof that the earth really does rotate? Make a note of the position of the pendulum, and come back again in an hour, or even two; the pendulum moves about 12 degrees per hour, so the change is very noticeable.

The Exploration of Space

A Scout C rocket, 23m (75ft) long, is aimed above your head, straight out the door. A German V2 rocket looks ominous, hanging from the ceiling. The Apollo 10 command module is surprisingly small in real life. This gallery explains the history and workings of rockets, from the 14kg (31lb) versions, fuelled by gunpowder, used by the British Army in 1806, up to the details of the giant Saturn V. The problems facing astronauts in space are also examined, plus what the surface of Mars looks like.

The Secret Life of the Home

This gallery in the basement is a fascinating technological guide to the modern home. It features an array of historic and current domestic appliances, gadgets and gizmos, with their use and workings explained.

Health Matters

An intriguing multimedia exhibition traces the story of modern medicine. You can even check out your lifestyle with an instant health check.

Launch Pad
This is the most popular place in the museum, requiring tickets on busy days. Children love this L-shaped space where they can reflect their voices across the room with sound dishes, change the shape and direction of 'lightning' in the plasma ball, and turn handles in the grain pit. Helpers are on hand to explain how things work. Try building a river bridge: it's not as easy as it looks.

Flight
History-making planes are here from the Vickers Vimy, the first plane to fly the Atlantic non-stop back in 1919, to the Gloster, built to test Frank Whittle's theories of jet propulsion. In Flight Lab, the science of flying is made easy to understand: Historic Ballooning is a computer game; the Whirling Arm illustrates how flaps control wing movement; movable models show the stressed skin concept of modern aircraft; and Harrier Flight tests your skills at vertical take-off and forward flight. There is plenty more to see, with special demonstrations and explanations by actors portraying characters from the past. Check the information desk for times of these and other events.

Exhibition Rd, SW7. Tel: 0870 870 4868; www.nmsi.ac.uk. Open: daily 10am–6pm. Closed: 24–26 Dec. Free admission; charge for special exhibitions. Tube: South Kensington.

Nearby attractions
Natural History Museum (*see pp80–81*).
Hyde Park and Kensington Gardens (*see p118*).
Victoria and Albert Museum (*see pp106–7*).

The Corliss steam engine

Saatchi Gallery

Now at the new venue of the Duke of York's HQ, this influential gallery shows changing exhibitions of contemporary art.
Kings Road, nr Sloane Square, SW3. www.saatchi-gallery.co.uk. Open: daily 10am–6pm. Free admission. Tube: Sloane Square.

Sir John Soane's Museum

Designed by architect Sir John Soane as a personal museum, this early 19th-century building is full of surprises. Nothing is quite straightforward; mirrors give an illusion of added space, panels in the Picture Room open to reveal hidden paintings and a view down into the Monk's Parlour, full of 'Gothick' oddities. The art collection alone is worth a visit, with works by Lawrence and Reynolds, Canaletto and Turner, and two series by Hogarth, *The Rake's Progress* and *The Election*.

The intention to leave the house 'as nearly as possible in the state in which Sir John Soane shall leave it' has been fulfilled. Colour schemes and objects appear as they were at the time of Soane's death in 1837.
13 Lincoln's Inn Fields, WC2. Tel: (020) 7405 2107. www.soane.org. Open: Tue–Sat 10am–5pm; also 6–9pm first Tue in month, when partially lit by candles. Free admission. Tube: Holborn.

Somerset House

Some claim this to be the first-ever government office block. If true, then it must be one of the most attractive. As well as august bodies like the Royal Academy of Arts and the Royal Society, this 18th-century behemoth has housed the Inland Revenue and the Navy (where Charles Dickens's father worked). In 1990, the Courtauld Galleries, including their famous collection of Impressionist paintings, moved here (*see p33*). It also houses the Gilbert Collection and the Hermitage Rooms.
The Strand, WC2. Tel: (020) 7845 4600. www.somerset-house.org.uk. Open: daily 10am–6pm. Tube: Temple (not on Sun), Covent Garden or Embankment.

Speakers' Corner

Britain's shrine to freedom of speech is relatively new. After a series of demonstrations in the 1870s, the right of assembly was granted at the northeast corner of Hyde Park, across from Marble Arch – so it is the listeners rather than the speakers who benefited. Now anyone can get on their 'soap box', as long as they are not obscene, blasphemous, treasonable, racist or

Fountains play in front of Somerset House

causing a breach of the peace. Do not expect fiery orators on Sunday mornings – some speakers are tedious!
Northeast corner of Hyde Park.
Open: best on Sun morning. Free admission. Tube: Marble Arch.

Staple Inn

Before the Great Fire, most of London must have looked like these houses. The heavily restored half-timbered row has survived since 1586, and was once a warehouse and marketplace for wool staplers or merchants.
Holborn, WC1. Courtyard only.
Open: Mon–Fri 8am–8pm.
Free admission. Tube: Chancery Lane.

Stock Exchange

The 'Footsie' (FTSE) started in 1984, but the 'Big Bang' in 1986 ended the separation of 'jobbers' from 'brokers'. Such jargon has always been an aspect of the London Stock Exchange, one of the world's leading financial institutions. Although this building is only a few years old, the history of the market goes back, like Lloyd's (*see p66*), to the 17th- and 18th-century coffee houses of the City of London. Then, as now, money had to be raised for business expansion and for new ventures; similarly, regulation has always been a vexed question. Back in 1697, legislation was passed 'to restrain the number of ill practices' – the most recent code dates from 1986, the Financial Services Act.
10 Paternoster Sq, EC4.
Tel: (020) 7797 1000.
Not open to the public.
Tube: St Paul's.

London, old and new

The Stock Exchange is on the right of this view from St Paul's Cathedral

The South Bank Centre

Covering 11 hectares (27 acres), this is the world's largest area devoted to the arts, and it dominates the south bank of the River Thames between Blackfriars and Westminster bridges. Every year millions enjoy the mixture of theatre, dance, music, poetry, art and film.

Once a wasteland site, development was triggered by the 1951 Festival of Britain, a post-war 'tonic to the nation'. Over 50 years on, the buildings are still some of the most unloved features of the London landscape. True, the Grade I listing of the Royal Festival Hall reflects its merits, but the Hayward Gallery and Queen Elizabeth Hall have been voted London's ugliest buildings.

The sites have been made more 'user-friendly' with exhibitions and free entertainment in the foyers, plus restaurants, cafés, bars and shops. In 2007, the Royal Festival Hall reopened after a lottery-funded major refurbishment. Further grandiose plans are afoot to redesign the whole complex.

Music

Opened in 1951, the **Royal Festival Hall** has 2,900 seats and has had full acoustic surgery enhancement. In 1992, the London Philharmonic became its first residential symphony orchestra, but the RFH is also used for jazz and dance. The **Queen Elizabeth Hall** (1,000 seats) and the **Purcell Room** (370) are used for solo recitals, chamber ensembles, folk and even cabaret acts.

Dance and mime

The **English National Ballet** has returned to the Royal Festival Hall after 11 years, while the **International Mime Festival** is a popular January event.

Poetry

The **Voice Box**, an intimate performance space on Level 5 of the RFH, caters for poetry reading.

The **Saison Poetry Library**, concentrating on modern British poetry, has manuscripts, videos and audio recordings.

Special events

Craft fairs are frequently held, as are painting exhibitions and musical performances, especially popular at weekends, on Level 2.

Unlovely outside, the South Bank Centre is a treasure trove within

Art

The flickering neon sculpture by Philip Vaughan and Roger Dainton signposts the **Hayward Gallery**, which stages temporary exhibitions. Its blockbuster successes have ranged from Toulouse-Lautrec to Andy Warhol. It covers classical and contemporary art, with British artists well represented.

Film

With its three screens, the **British Film Institute Southbank** offers a lively daily programme of films old and new, with themed seasons highlighting special actors or directors. The London Film Festival is based here each October.

National Theatre

In the 18th century, actor David Garrick suggested a National Company; it finally started in 1963 and moved here 13 years later.

There are three theatres: the **Lyttelton** has the traditional proscenium stage, the **Olivier**, the largest, has an open stage, and the **Cottesloe** is an adaptable studio space. Since British actors are not pigeonholed as 'stage' or 'screen', major stars frequently appear.

A backstage tour provides a glimpse of the working world of actors, lighting technicians and stage managers (*see p149 for details*).

Royal Festival Hall, Queen Elizabeth Hall, Purcell Room, Voice Box and Hayward Gallery, general information and bookings: Tel: 0871 663 2500.
www.nationaltheatre.org.uk.
British Film Insititute:
Tel: (020) 7928 3232.
www.southbankcentre.co.uk.
National Theatre: Tel: (020) 7452 3000.
www.bfi.org.uk.
Tube: Waterloo.

Tate Galleries

What could be better than replacing a grim prison with one of the world's great art collections? Down went Millbank Prison, and up went Sir Henry Tate's gallery, given to the nation in 1897 to hold his collection of contemporary British painting and sculpture. More British works, from the 16th century onwards, were added from the National Gallery, including the entire collection of the Turner Bequest.

Tate Britain

In 1917, the Tate Gallery (as it was known until 2000) expanded its scope to include the collection of modern French art bequeathed to it by Sir Hugh Lane, and thus Tate also started a national collection of modern foreign art. A few years later, the great central sculpture galleries were added on.

In 1987, a new east wing, the Clore Gallery, was opened. This was designed by the eminent architect James Stirling specifically to hold and display the Turner Bequest – 300 paintings and 30,000 drawings and watercolours left to the nation by the industrious JMW Turner.

Innovative director Nicholas Serota rehung the rest of the gallery in 1990 in chronological order, tracing the development of British art from 1550 to the present day, as well as showing the connections between British and foreign art in the 20th century – the parallel developments in the Schools of New York, Paris and Continental Europe. In this way, the rigid division between historic (pre-1900) and modern (post-1900) art was broken.

The Bloomsbury Group, Vorticism, the Abstract and Expressionist movements and Pop Art are well represented. The Tate owns Roy Lichtenstein's *Whaam!* and Andy Warhol's *Marilyn Diptych*. Its eclectic displays have included such surprises as a hanging upside-down Christmas tree. The Tate has a reputation, stoked by the popular press, of shocking its audiences. Londoners still talk about the bricks in Carl Andre's *Equivalent VIII*, acquired in 1972, which consisted of 120 bricks piled on the floor in two symmetrical layers.

The opening of the Centenary Development in 2001 added several new galleries to Tate Britain. The gallery now houses the National Collection of Historic British Paintings (from the 16th century to the present day) and the National Collection of

Modern Art, which includes foreign paintings and sculptures.
Millbank, SW1. Tel: (020) 7887 8888; (020) 7887 8008 for recorded information. www.tate.org.uk/britain.
Open: daily 10am–5.50pm.
Free admission, but charge for special exhibitions. Free tours.
Tube: Pimlico.

Tate Modern

In the 1990s the Tate trustees acquired the disused Bankside Power Station in Southwark – a monumental 20th-century building, opposite St Paul's Cathedral. The former Turbine Hall now marks a breathtaking entrance to the gallery, and at the top of the building is a new two-storey glass roof which provides natural light into the galleries on the top floors, and also houses a stunning café.

Moving part of the former Tate Gallery's modern collection into this newly adapted space, Tate Modern opened to the public in 2000 as the home of international 20th- and 21st-century modern art. It includes major works by Dalí, Picasso, Matisse, Rothko and Warhol, as well as contemporary artists such as Dorothy Cross, Gilbert & George and Susan Hiller. In its first 100 days, it welcomed two million visitors!
Bankside, SE1. Tel: (020) 7887 8888. www.tate.org.uk/modern.
Open: daily 10am–6pm (10pm on Fri & Sat). Free admission; charge for special exhibitions. Tube: Southwark or Blackfriars.

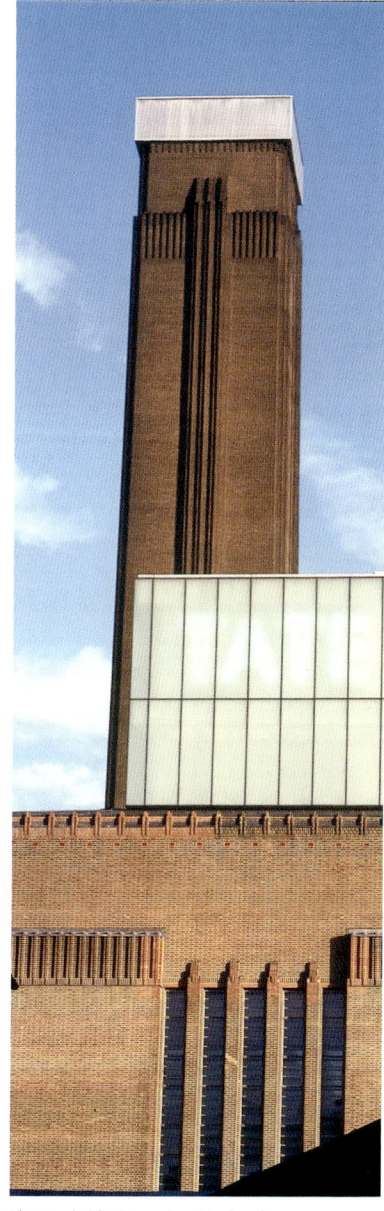

The Bankside Power Station has been reincarnated as the Tate Modern art gallery

Temple Bar

A defiant dragon (or 'griffin') stands on this boundary between the City and Westminster. Traditionally, the monarch stops here until given permission to enter the City by the Lord Mayor.
The Strand, WC2. Tube: Temple.

Temple, Middle and Inner

These Inns of Court were named after the Knights Templars, a militaristic monastic order who protected pilgrims, and fought to keep the Holy Land under Christian rule. The Templars were disbanded in 1312, their land eventually passing to lawyers in the 15th century.

Temple Church, in Pump Court, is supposedly based on the Holy Sepulchre Church in Jerusalem, and dates from 1185. The crossed legs of stone effigies like Sir Geoffrey de Mandeville's (d.1144) are thought to show participation in the crusades.

Middle Temple Hall, opened in 1576, has portraits of kings and queens above the High Table (made from a single oak tree). In front stands Drake's Table, reputedly made from a hatch on the *Golden Hinde*, the ship that circumnavigated the world between 1577 and 1580. Shakespeare's *Twelfth Night* was first performed here in 1602.
Middle Temple Hall. Middle Temple Lane, EC4. Tel: (020) 7427 4800. Open: daily 8am–7pm.
Temple Church. Tel: (020) 7353 8559. Open: generally daily but check website (www.templechurch.com) 1–4pm, Sun for services. Free admission. The public are allowed into the courtyards and alleys as well as Temple Church and Middle Temple Hall. The gardens, however, are private. Tube: Temple.

Thames Barrier

Flooding has always threatened London, the current danger coming from surge tides funnelling water up the Thames. In 1984, the world's largest movable flood barrier was inaugurated at Woolwich Reach. Seven stainless-steel shells span the 520m (570yds) width of river; between these are gates which are five storeys high, heavier than a naval destroyer, and take 30 minutes to raise. The visitor centre explains all. The best time to visit is when the gates are being raised – visitors should telephone in advance for schedule of dates.
Unity Way, Woolwich, SE18.
Tel: (020) 8305 4188. Open: Apr–Sept daily 10.30am–4.30pm; Oct–Mar daily 11am–3.30pm. Admission charge.
By river boat: from Westminster or Greenwich Pier.

Part of the Thames Barrier at Woolwich

Tower Bridge

One of London's best-known landmarks, this fanciful feat of Victorian engineering was completed in 1894, and opened with great ceremony. Although clad in granite and Portland stone, the bridge is made of steel. So that ocean-going ships could make their way upstream, the central section was built to be raised, creating a 60m (65yd) space for passage. Tower Bridge was lifted 6,160 times in its first year of operation. Nowadays, the bridge is still raised, but only about 500 times a year. The original machinery remains, however, and can be seen in the engine room.

Inside the bridge a high-tech exhibition uses animatronic figures, atmospheric tableaux, videos and special effects to re-create the era when the bridge was built.

From the high-level walkways (43m/50yds tall) which link the two towers, only the birds have better views of London: upstream to St Paul's and the Houses of Parliament, downstream to Canary Wharf in Docklands.
Tower Bridge, SE1. Tel: (020) 7403 3761. www.towerbridge. org.uk. Open: Apr–Sept daily 10am–6.30pm; Oct–Mar daily 9.30am–6pm. 1½ hour tour. Closed: 24–26 Dec. Admission charge. Tube: Tower Hill or London Bridge.

Tower Bridge, a fairy-tale structure

Walk: Theatreland and Bohemian London

London's West End is known for its famous theatres, its lively nightlife and its numerous places to eat, drink and be merry.

Allow 1 hour.

Start at Piccadilly Circus underground station. Exit via subway 4, on to Coventry St.

1 Piccadilly Circus
Always busy, this is where the first large electric signs flashed a hundred years ago. The statue of Eros has been moved during the last century to ease traffic congestion. Behind it, the Criterion Brasserie restaurant has a glistening mosaic ceiling (1870) like a Viennese coffee house. Next door, another former theatre, the Trocadero, is now an entertainment, dining and shopping complex.
Walk straight through the Trocadero to Shaftesbury Ave and turn right.

2 Shaftesbury Avenue
The Lyric Theatre and its companions, the Apollo, Gielgud and Queen's theatres, are the heart of 'Theatreland'. *Turn left on to Wardour St.*

3 Soho
The name dates back many centuries to the cry of fox hunters, but Soho's reputation as a 'foreign' enclave is 300 years old. Although a 'red light' district, cafés, clubs and restaurants

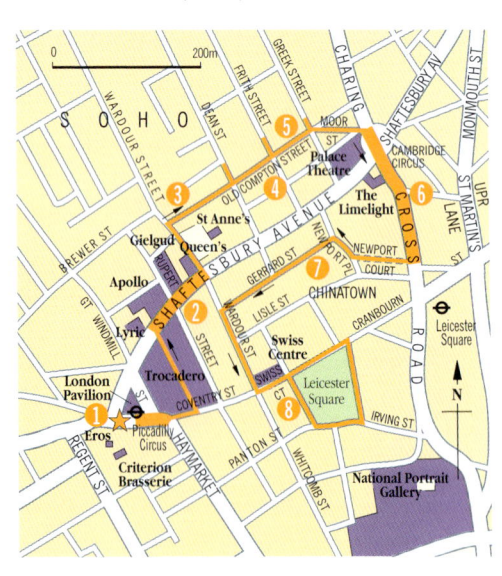

now cater for the film, TV and video industry concentrated here.
Turn right into Old Compton St.

4 Old Compton Street
Always Bohemian, this is also the heart of London's gay community.
Continue along Old Compton St, with optional 'dips' into streets on the left.

5 Dean Street, Frith Street and Greek Street
Soho has always drawn foreigners. Karl Marx lived above the restaurant at No 26 Dean Street; Mozart lived in Frith Street, opposite the jazz lovers' favourite club, Ronnie Scott's (No 47).
At the Three Greyhounds pub on Old Compton St, take Moor St to Cambridge Circus. Cross Shaftesbury Ave and go down Charing Cross Rd.

6 Charing Cross Road
A converted church is now a branch of the Australian-themed Walkabout pub; across the road specialist bookshops attract browsers. Unfortunately for fans of the film *84 Charing Cross Road*, that site lost out to developers.
Turn right up Newport Court, and then left into Gerrard St.

7 Chinatown
Chinese restaurants and shops were here long before the 1980s brought a red-and-gold gateway, stone lions and dual-language street signs to make Gerrard Street the centre of London's lively Chinatown.
Turn left into Wardour St and left again into Swiss Court.

8 Leicester Square
The modern Swiss Centre is a piece of Switzerland in London, complete with jolly automated glockenspiel. To mark the nation's 700th birthday in 1991, the paved area outside was renamed Swiss Court.

Bordered by cinemas, Leicester Square has been a centre of entertainment for 150 years. The square now has busts of artists and writers. The Half-Price Tkts booth is on the lower end of the square.
Use either Piccadilly Circus or Leicester Square underground stations.

Charlie Chaplin in Leicester Square

Walk: Theatreland and Bohemian London

The Tower of London

When Londoners say 'The Tower', they mean all of its 7.3 hectares (18 acres), and all the sights within, from the ravens to the Chapel Royal, and from the Yeoman Warders to the Crown Jewels. There are 20 towers in all, but originally 'The Tower' was just the White Tower, built by William the Conqueror to reinforce his authority over a defeated people. Subsequent monarchs increased the size and defences for protection against their subjects, both noble and common.

The Tower was also a magnificent palace in its heyday, housing some 1,000 people; today it is home to 150. The guns are only for ceremonies now, but when the Tower is floodlit at night, there is an eerie sense of the past. Its story encompasses not just the history of London but the history of the country as well.

The White Tower

William the Conqueror chose a strategic site for the tower, a V between the Thames and the old Roman wall. Standing 27.4m (90ft) high and with walls 4.6m (15ft) thick at the base, the pale Kentish grey and whiter Norman limestone would have gleamed with whitewash – hence the name. Over the years, this has been used as an armoury, a wardrobe and a storehouse for jewels. In the 18th century, even public records were kept here; but a Norman atmosphere remains in the now spartan St John's Chapel, originally rich with colour and gold decoration.

The Queen's House

Henry VIII's wives were kept here – the second, Anne Boleyn, and the fifth, Catherine Howard. Both were beheaded, but it is Anne's ghost that supposedly walks at night. Guy Fawkes was tortured and interrogated here after the plot to blow up Parliament was discovered in November 1605.

The Bloody Tower

The Young Princes, the 12-year-old boy King Edward V and his 10-year-old brother, the Duke of York, were imprisoned here. They disappeared in August 1483, supposedly murdered by order of Richard III, one of the least loved of kings.

Tower Green

Only the privileged were beheaded in the privacy of the Tower, rather than in front of raucous crowds on Tower Hill.

A marker commemorates those who died here, including the Nine-Day Queen, Lady Jane Grey, aged only 16.

The Chapel Royal of St Peter ad Vincula

Some famous prisoners are buried here, including three queens.

The Jewel House

The display area includes an exhibition about past monarchs. The traditional Coronation Crown of St Edward was too heavy for Queen Victoria. She commissioned the lighter Imperial State Crown, sparkling with 3,174 jewels and the Second Star of Africa. At 317 carats this is second only to the 530-carat First Star of Africa, the world's largest cut diamond, which sits atop the sceptre made for Charles II.

The Royal Armouries

In this priceless collection, as well as weapons and armour from the time of the Saxons and Vikings to those of the Gulf War, there are implements of torture and punishment.

Ravens and Yeoman Warders

These are the symbols of the Tower of London. According to legend, both England and the Tower will fall if the ravens fly away, so their wings are clipped. The half-hourly tours given by the Yeoman Warders in their Tudor-style uniforms are a must.
Tower Hill, EC3. Tel: (020) 3166 6311. www.hrp.org.uk. Open: daily Mar–Oct, Tue–Sat 9am–5.30pm, Sun & Mon 10am–5.30pm; Nov–Feb, Tue–Sat 9am–4.30pm, Sun & Mon 10am–4.30pm. Admission charge. Tube: Tower Hill.

The White Tower, part of the huge Tower of London site

All around the Tower

The Tower of London is the heart of one of the most interesting areas of the city. From the Tower Bridge walkway (see p97) you can see 2,000 years of history, from Roman relics to World War II warship HMS Belfast. Do not forget the ancient ceremonies that make a visit to the Tower unforgettable, including the Ceremony of the Keys and Beating the Bounds.

Roman Wall

Try to forget the presence of today's traffic; 1,700 years ago this was an impressive and effective defence.
Tube: Tower Hill.

Trinity Square Gardens

Look for the marker showing the site of the scaffold for public executions. The last man to be beheaded in Britain was Lord Lovat, one of the

Some of the dazzling creations on show at the Fashion and Textile Museum in Bermondsey Street

Scottish rebel lords. He was executed here in 1747.

North side of the river
All Hallows by the Tower

This medieval church has American connections, including the baptism of William Penn and the marriage of John Quincy Adams (6th US president).
Byward St, EC3. Tel: (020) 7481 2928.
www.allhallowsbythetower.org.uk.
Open: Mon–Fri 8am–6pm, Sat & Sun 10am–5pm (closed during services).
Free admission, but charge for Undercroft Museum.
Tube: Tower Hill.

All Hallows Brass Rubbing Centre

Particularly enjoyable for children; visitors can make their own souvenir brass rubbings here.
Address and phone as above. Open: daily 11am–4.30pm (except during services). Charge for rubbing.

South side of the river
Design Museum

The brainchild of Sir Terence Conran of Habitat fame, this museum opened in 1989 with the aim of making the public aware of everyday objects, from pens to telephones, and from chairs to kettles. Design successes and failures are shown, while video games challenge the visitor.
28 Shad Thames, SE1.
Tel: (020) 7403 6933.
www.designmuseum.org. Open: daily 10am–5.45pm. Admission charge.
Tube: Tower Hill or London Bridge.

HMS *Belfast*

This 10,722-tonne cruiser is the largest surviving World War II warship in Europe. She once carried a crew of 800 on her seven decks, and her guns could bombard shore targets as far as 22km (13$^{1}/_{2}$ miles) away. The ship is now a museum commemorating the bravery of sailors in war.
Morgan's Lane, Tooley St (via Hays Galleria), SE1. Tel: (020) 7940 6300.
http://hmsbelfast.iwm.org.uk.
Bridge open: Mar–Oct, daily 10am–6pm; Nov–Feb closes 5pm.
Closed: 24–26 Dec.
Admission charge. Tube: Tower Hill (then ferry: frequent in summer, restricted in winter), or London Bridge.

CEREMONIES AT THE TOWER OF LONDON

At 9.30pm the **Ceremony of the Keys** begins. In this 700-year-old nightly ritual, the gates are locked and the keys handed to the Chief Yeoman Warder as 'God preserve Queen Elizabeth' rings out. To watch it, apply in writing to the Resident Governor, two–three months in advance.

Royal Gun Salutes mark royal birthdays, Accession Day and Coronation Day. A 62-gun salute is fired at the Tower of London at 1pm to mark the anniversary of the Accession. There are 41-gun salutes for **Trooping the Colour** and the **State Opening of Parliament**.

Beating the Bounds dates back to medieval times. It defined the boundaries of each London parish. Once every three years (next in 2011) on Ascension Day, choirboys beat the 31 boundaries with willow canes.

Walk: Bards and bawds

One of London's fastest changing areas is at the southern end of London Bridge. Once famous for bear-baiting and Shakespeare's plays, brothels and brewing, this area is now an intriguing mix of old buildings, new office blocks and attractive pubs.

Allow 1 hour.

From London Bridge station, cross the green footbridge at the end of the forecourt, marked 'To Guy's Hospital and St Thomas Street'. At the foot of the steps turn sharp left and left again into St Thomas St.

1 Guy's Hospital
The statue in the forecourt on the left commemorates Thomas Guy, the wealthy publisher who founded this world-famous teaching hospital in 1726. In the square red-brick tower opposite is a 19th-century operating theatre, now a museum (*see pp66–7*).
Turn left on to Borough High St.

2 The George Inn
Borough High Street is lined with little yards which once housed inns like Chaucer's Tabard (Talbot Yard), and Shakespeare's and Dickens' White Hart (White Hart Yard). The George Inn is the only survivor, rebuilt after the Great Fire of London in 1676. Shakespeare was another regular visitor.
Leave George Inn Yard and cross Borough High St and Southwark St to enter Stoney St.

3 Borough Market
One of London's lively farmers' and wholesale markets, open only on Thursday, Friday and Saturday.
Turn left on to Park St, and follow in a curve under Southwark Bridge. Turn right into Bear Gardens.

4 Shakespeare's Globe Theatre
The 'rebuilding' of Shakespeare's Globe was the ambition of the late American theatre director Sam Wanamaker. His dream became a reality when it opened in 1997. An exhibition here holds reminders that four theatres, including Shakespeare's original Globe, made this London's 17th-century Broadway.
Turn left at the end of Bear Gardens.

5 Wren's House
A plaque on No 49 claims that Sir Christopher Wren lived here while

supervising the construction of St Paul's Cathedral. The imposing building ahead is the Tate Modern, a treasure house of modern art (*see p95*).
Retrace your steps and follow the riverside walk under Southwark Bridge. Next to the old Anchor pub, enter Clink St.

6 Clink Street

Clink Street's notorious prison gave rise to the slang expression 'in the clink', meaning 'in prison'. Ironically, all the illicit entertainment banished from the City flourished right in the shadow of the now ruined Bishop of Winchester's palace!
Continue to the end of Clink St.

7 *Golden Hinde*

In St Mary Overy Dock is the *Golden Hinde*, a replica of the square-rigged galleon in which Sir Francis Drake circumnavigated the world from 1577–80.
Leave the dock and go along Cathedral St to Southwark Cathedral.

8 Southwark Cathedral

Dating back some 700 years, St Saviour's Church was given cathedral status in 1905. Among the many monuments inside is one to John Harvard, founder of the American university, who was baptised here.
Continue via Montague Cl to Tooley St.

9 The London Dungeon

London's museum of torture and execution (*see p66*).
Continue to Hay's Galleria.

10 Hay's Galleria

A soaring glass roof joins two former warehouses. Underneath is a plaza of shops and restaurants.
To cross the river, either walk along the riverside path, going over London Bridge, or return to London Bridge station.

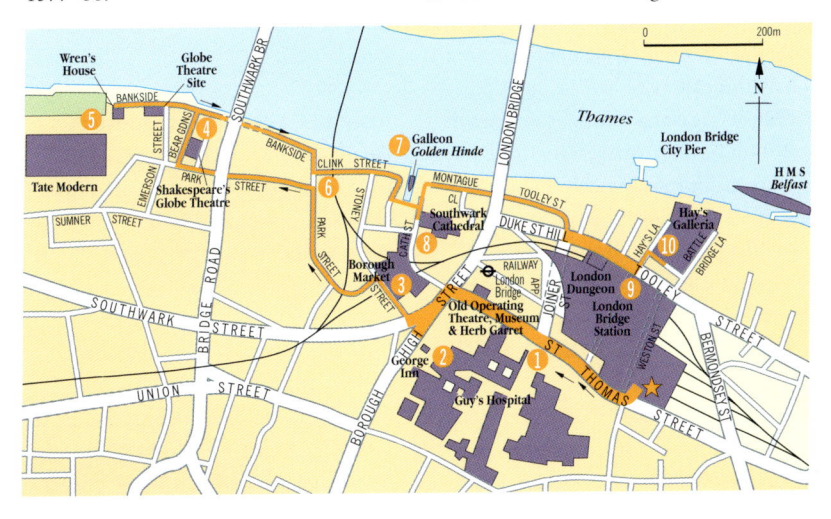

Victoria and Albert Museum

From its crown-like dome dominating South Kensington, to the statues of Inspiration and Knowledge over the doorway, this is a statement of Victorian ideals. The V & A is dedicated to applied art and design. It is not full of Victoriana, although it was a spin-off from the Great Exhibition of 1851. Today the 11km (7 miles) of galleries display objects from all over the world, from different ages and cultures.

Major changes in the last few years range from splendid new galleries of Indian, Chinese and Japanese art to the redesigned Raphael Gallery and Silver Galleries. The garden has been redesigned, as has the Italianate courtyard which is now an elegant meeting point. A wide range of events and workshops are regularly held in the museum.

Medieval Treasury

Directly in front of the main entrance hall, this gallery's low-level lighting protects treasures dating from the 4th to 14th century. Many were made for religious purposes: richly coloured stained glass, a delicately carved ivory Madonna and Child, and a bishop's cope (cloak) covered with threads of gold, silver and silk, made by professional embroiderers.

Raphael Gallery

This displays the seven tapestry cartoons completed by Raphael in 1516. The designs on paper of tapestries for the Sistine Chapel represent one of the most important surviving examples of Renaissance art in the world.

The TT Tsui Gallery of Chinese Art

Opened in 1991, this gallery explains the design, function and symbolism of Chinese objects. Go ahead, you're allowed to touch the head made of serpentine and the Ming dynasty vase!

Toshiba Gallery of Japanese Art

Wooden beams create the feel of a Japanese house. Nowadays, kimonos, porcelain and lacquer boxes are familiar examples of Japanese craftsmanship. The suits of armour, however, come as a shock. Made of iron, leather, gold-lacquering, silk and even polished rayfish skin, these are topped with iron helmets, and look frightening, even locked in glass cases.

The Cast Courts

Imagine what an impression this gallery made back in the late 19th century when few people travelled abroad. How they must have stared at the detail of the Porta de la Gloria, the famous west entrance of the church of pilgrims in Santiago de Compostela. Originally made for art students, these fragile plaster casts are a valuable record of originals that have since been damaged by pollution and war.

The Nehru Gallery of Indian Art

The British continue to be fascinated by India, and although this gallery reflects the influences of invaders and conquerors, it also shows how Indian art was prized by Europeans, for whom the carved ivory, jade and patterned textiles were both romantic and exotic.

Dress collection

One wonders how wealthy ladies managed to enter doors and carriages in the elaborately hooped gowns of the 18th century. Follow the fashion, from the flapper to Vivienne Westwood.

Glass Gallery

This redesigned gallery illustrates the history of glass over 4,000 years, with 7,000 pieces from Europe, America and the Middle East exhibited.

These are only a few of the marvels to see; others include the **20th-Century Galleries**, the **Samsung Gallery of Korean Art** and the **European Ornament Gallery**. Some of the latter gallery's collection may appear in other areas of the museum.

Cromwell Rd, SW7. Tel: (020) 7942 2000. www.vam.ac.uk. Open: daily 10am–5.45pm. Late viewing on Fri until 10pm. Closed: 24–26 Dec. Free admission; charge for special exhibitions. Tube: South Kensington.

The main entrance of the museum with its spectacular blown-glass chandelier

Walk: Victoria and Albert

Kensington, made a Royal Borough at Queen Victoria's request in 1901, shows the influence of this monarch and her husband, Prince Albert.

Allow 1 hour.

Start at High St Kensington underground station. Turn right and follow Kensington High St. Past the Royal Garden Hotel turn left on to Palace Avenue, and at Kensington Palace turn right into Kensington Gardens.

1 Kensington Palace

William and Mary's Wren-designed home where several members of the Royal Family have apartments. The late Diana, Princess of Wales, used to live here. It was here that the 18-year-old Princess Victoria learned that she had become Queen of England.

2 Kensington Gardens

This is just a taste of this huge park, with hills, ponds, oaks and chestnuts.
Follow the path between the Round Pond and the bandstand, and take the right turn for the Albert Memorial.

3 Albert Memorial

Recent extensive restoration has returned this 53m- (174ft-) high monument to its former glory. It is densely decorated with symbols of the life and interests of Prince Albert, whose pet project, the Great Exhibition of 1851, drew six million visitors to Hyde Park.
Walk around the Memorial, go down the steps and cross Kensington Gore to the Royal Albert Hall.

4 Royal Albert Hall

This 5,000-seat concert hall opened in 1871. Concerts, sport tournaments, conferences and gala dinners have been held here. In summer the Promenade Concerts (the 'Proms') are held, taking their name from the promenaders who buy cheaper tickets and remain standing.
Walk anticlockwise around the hall, past the modern Royal College of Art and the decorated Royal College of Organists. Opposite entrance 13/14 go down the steps to Prince Consort Rd.

5 The Colleges

Prince Albert wanted to group together institutes of higher education and

museums to bring learning to the masses. In a row are: the Royal College of Music, the former Royal School of Mines, the former City and Guilds Institute. These buildings are now part of the world-famous Imperial College of Science, Technology and Medicine.
Turn left along Prince Consort Rd to reach Exhibition Rd. Cross over here and enter Prince's Gardens.

6 Victorian legacy
The development around Exhibition Road after 1851 included tall houses, fine squares and small mews.
At the bottom of the hill a gate leads to the path circling the graveyard of Holy Trinity Church. Go past the church, down the side of the London Oratory, and turn right on Thurloe Place.

7 The London Oratory
This Italianate building became Britain's leading centre for Roman Catholics when it opened 125 years ago. Latin Mass is held several times a week.
Continue along Thurloe Place.

8 The Victoria and Albert Museum and the Natural History Museum
The V & A had a facelift in 1991, revealing statues of Turner and Constable, Hogarth and Reynolds. Across Exhibition Road the Natural History Museum and Science Museum fulfil Prince Albert's dream of bringing science to the people.
Cross Exhibition Rd for the entrance to South Kensington underground station.

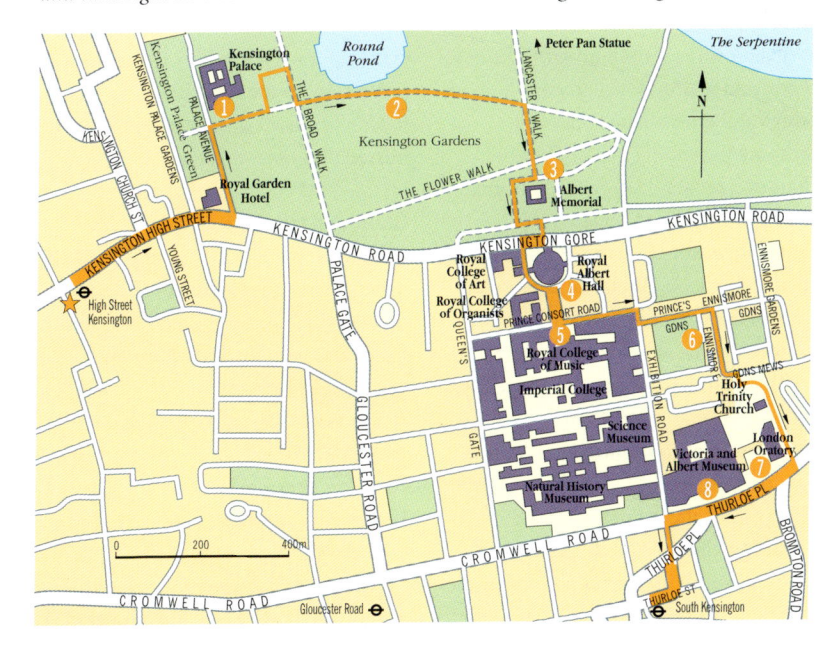

Westminster Abbey

The embodiment of English history, the abbey has been the site of every coronation (apart from Edward V and Edward VIII) since that of William the Conqueror in 1066. Officially called the Collegiate Church of St Peter, this was an abbey for Benedictine monks for 600 years until the Dissolution of the Monasteries of 1540. What we see today is largely the result of Henry III's enthusiastic rebuilding in the second half of the 13th century.

Very French, with an unusually high nave (30m/98ft) and unity of style, the only major additions have been the beautiful Lady Chapel or Henry VII Chapel (16th century) and the West Towers designed by Sir Christopher Wren and his assistant, Nicholas Hawksmoor (18th century).

Inside, funeral monuments fill every nook and cranny. Once the privilege of kings and queens, the abbey has become the resting place of national figures since the 18th century. Regular services and vibrant ceremonies, however, ensure that the abbey is more than a museum. Above all, it is a place of worship, and the best way to appreciate the abbey is to come twice, once as a tourist, then during a service.

The Tomb of the Unknown Warrior

At the west end of the nave, just beyond the plain stone exhorting 'Remember Winston Churchill', is the simple, moving tomb of an unidentified soldier interred on 11 November 1920, along with soil from the battlefields of France. He represents the 765,399 British servicemen who fell in World War I. The US Congressional Medal of Honor (awarded in 1921) is on a nearby pillar, as is the flag that covered the coffin.

On the right (facing inwards), outside the Chapel of St George, is a contemporary portrait of Richard II; further up on the left, playwright Ben Jonson is buried upright with his name misspelt on his tombstone.

Choir and transept

The gilded choir screen with tributes to great scientists is Victorian, and the organ, rebuilt and enlarged since 1730, has been played by such distinguished organists as Henry Purcell.

The south side of the transept is best known for Poets' Corner. Ever since Chaucer, who worked in the abbey, was buried here in 1400, many of Britain's greatest writers have been interred or honoured here. However, Shakespeare had to wait until 1740, Burns until

Gothic architecture at its most spectacular

1885, and Blake waited for 100 years until 1957.

Across the nave is Statesmen's Corner with memorials to numerous prime ministers. This was the former royal entrance to the abbey, through the heavily carved Solomon's Porch.

The sanctuary

This is the actual site of coronations, seen on television in 1953 when the Archbishop of Canterbury placed the crown on the head of Queen Elizabeth II. The Coronation Chair is kept in the shrine of Edward the Confessor, the most sacred part of the abbey, and still a destination for pilgrims. King Edward's Chair, made of English oak, was first used for Edward II's coronation in 1307.

Lady Chapel

Better known as Henry VII Chapel, this is among the most beautiful buildings in the world, thanks to the lace-like tracery that soars above the tombs and burial places of Henry VII, Edward VI, Mary I, Elizabeth I, Mary Queen of Scots and James I.

Westminster Abbey Museum

Together with the Chapter House and Pyx Chamber, the museum in the undercroft adds to an appreciation of British history. As well as replicas of coronation regalia and armour, funeral effigies of Henry VII, Charles II (in garter robes) and even Lord Nelson give a sense of what these famous people really looked like.

Westminster Abbey, SW1.
Tel: (020) 7222 5152 for details of regular and special services.
www.westminster-abbey.org.
Open: Mon–Fri 9.30am–4.30pm (last entry), Sat 9.30am–2.30pm (last entry), Sun for services only. Opening hours sometimes vary so check the website for up to date details.
Admission charge.
Chapter House, Abbey Museum & Pyx Chamber are open daily 10.30am–4pm.

Tours to special areas: Apr–Sept weekdays 10am, 10.30am, 11am, 2pm & 2.30pm, Sat 10am, 10.30am & 11am; Oct–Mar weekdays 10.30am, 11am, 2pm & 2.30pm, Sat 10.30am & 11am.
Admission charge.

Westminster and Parliament

In Britain, 'Westminster' means government and this has been the site of council meetings and parliamentary gatherings since 1265. Today's Houses of Parliament, replacing earlier buildings destroyed by fire in 1834, were built to the Victorian Gothic design of Charles Barry and Augustus Pugin. This home of the Mother of Parliaments is divided into upper and lower houses, a concept that has been copied by democracies around the world.

Houses of Parliament
To appreciate the grandeur of the building, view it from Westminster Bridge or from the south bank of the Thames. The 266m- (290yd-) long façade, dense with statues, hides 3 hectares (7½ acres) of rooms linked by 3km (1¾ miles) of passages and 100 staircases.

Big Ben
The 96m- (315ft-) high tower is not named after the clock, but after the 13.5-tonne bell that heralds the hour and, thanks to the BBC World Service, is heard all over the world. Each clock face is 7m (23ft) across with minute hands 4.27m (14ft) long, travelling over 160km (100 miles) a year.

House of Commons
Television coverage has made familiar the long green benches, wigged Speaker, and clamorous Members of Parliament (MPs). A full house is a cramped place: 646 MPs are elected, but there are only seats for 437. In front of the Speaker (who controls the House) is a table with dispatch boxes and the mace of office. To his/her left is the party in power, the Government; to his/her right, Her Majesty's Loyal Opposition, who are always eager to disagree.

Red lines on the floor divide the two parties, a relic of the days when members were kept two swords' lengths apart for safety's sake. By tradition the monarch has been forbidden to enter the House of Commons ever since 1642, when Charles I burst in, in order to arrest members who opposed him.
Tel: 0870 906 3773. www.parliament.uk. Open: July–Sept Mon–Sat for tours. Admission charge.

Westminster Hall
Medieval carpentry made a technological leap forward with the self-supporting hammerbeam roof in this, the only surviving part of the 11th-century Palace of Westminster.

Used for parliamentary sessions, banquets, and the trials of Anne Boleyn, Guy Fawkes and Charles I, it was also here that Sir Winston Churchill's body lay in state in 1965.

House of Lords

Television's entry into the gilded splendour of the House of Lords revealed many peers apparently snoozing. In fact, their Lordships are listening to loudspeakers in the back of the red leather benches. Only some of the 735 peers and bishops (who are eligible to attend) turn out regularly to debate major issues of the day.

Under the steady gaze of the 18 statues of the barons who witnessed the signing of Magna Carta is the Lord Chancellor sitting on the Woolsack, which takes its name from England's prosperous wool trade 600 years ago. *See House of Commons for visiting information.*

Victoria Tower

An impressive 3 million documents are stored here, including every Act of Parliament since 1497. The Union Flag flies when parliament is in session. The Victoria Tower Gardens along the river feature the *Burghers of Calais* sculpture by Rodin, and a memorial to the Emancipation of Slaves in 1834.

Jewel Tower

Opposite the Victoria Tower is the 14th-century, L-shaped Jewel Tower which houses a permanent on the history of Parliame

Parliament Square

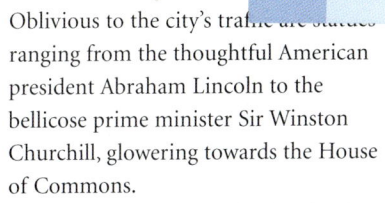

Oblivious to the city's traffic are statues ranging from the thoughtful American president Abraham Lincoln to the bellicose prime minister Sir Winston Churchill, glowering towards the House of Commons.

St Margaret's, the parish church of the House of Commons since 1614, is where Catherine of Aragon was to marry Prince Arthur. He died a few months after the wedding. She later married his younger brother, Henry VIII. The church also holds the grave of Sir Walter Raleigh. The Elizabethan explorer and writer was beheaded in Old Palace Yard and buried beneath the altar.

Parliamentary sessions may be viewed from the Visitors' Gallery of each House from Mon–Thur and on sitting Fridays. Queues form outside St Stephen's entrance; expect a one- to two-hour wait for the House of Commons, less for the House of Lords. Tube: Westminster.

The Houses of Parliament occupy an ancient site on the north bank of the River Thames

Whitehall and Trafalgar Square

One of the best views of London is from the porticoed entrance of the National Gallery. Across Trafalgar Square, you can pick out Nelson's Column, Whitehall and, in the distance, Big Ben.

Trafalgar Square

Named after Nelson's final and most famous naval victory over the French in 1805, the square was completed in 1845. Huge fountains, dating from 1936, gush forth each morning. The original fountains now stand outside Parliament in Ottawa, Canada.

Before New Year's Eve the fountains are drained, to prevent possible drownings by drunken revellers. Each Christmas, a towering tree arrives from Norway, a gift of thanks to the British people for their help during World War II.

Pigeon numbers have been drastically reduced since a phased feeding programme was introduced in 2003 by the last mayor, Ken Livingstone.

Nelson's Column

Thirty-eight years after Admiral Lord Nelson was killed at the Battle of Trafalgar, his statue was placed on the 52m- (170ft-) high column. The bas-reliefs at the base were made from melted-down French cannons to commemorate his victories. Sir Edwin Landseer's lions were added in 1867.

The Banqueting House is the only remnant of the Palace of Whitehall

Charles I statue
On a triangular island, cut off by traffic from Trafalgar Square and Whitehall, a mounted Charles I stares down Whitehall towards the site of his execution. Behind the statue, a tablet marks the point from which all distances to London are measured.

Whitehall
A long street joining Trafalgar Square to Parliament Square where Whitehall Palace once stood, 'Whitehall' is now synonymous with government ministries and their bureaucracy.

Old Admiralty
On the west side, a stately entrance with two flying horses marks the former headquarters from which Britain once ruled the waves.

Horse Guards
The daily Mounting of the Guard by the troopers dates back to when this gateway led to Whitehall Palace, which burnt down in 1698. Wearing red plumes and blue tunics (the Blues and Royals), or white plumes with red tunics (the Life Guards), the straight-faced troopers tolerate photographers.

Through the arch is a huge parade ground, more commonly known as Horse Guards Parade, site of the annual summer spectaculars, Trooping the Colour (see p28) and Beating the Retreat.
Mounting of the Guard
Weekdays at 11am, Sun at 10am.

Banqueting House
This is all that remains of the Palace of Whitehall, the primary London residence of monarchs from Henry VIII until 1698 when it burnt down. The Banqueting House, completed for James I in 1622 to Inigo Jones's design, is renowned for its magnificent ceiling, painted by Rubens. The artist was commissioned by Charles I, who, in 1649, was executed in public on a scaffold above the present entrance. So ended the divine right of kings to govern as they liked.

Further down is a statue of Sir Walter Raleigh, in plumed hat and high boots, and 'Monty', Field Marshal Viscount Montgomery, sporting his signature beret.
The Banqueting House, Whitehall, SW1.
Tel: 0203 166 6154. www.hrp.org.uk.
Open: Mon–Sat 10am–5pm.
Admission charge.
Tube: Charing Cross or Westminster.

Downing Street
The home of the Prime Minister is traditionally at No 10, and the Chancellor of the Exchequer at No 11 (see p58).

The Cenotaph
A plain memorial in the middle of the road is the focus of the nation on Remembrance Sunday each November when the Royal Family, politicians, the armed forces, and veterans pay tribute to the war dead.

London's lungs

The parks of London were an important part of the city as far back as the 18th century, when the phrase 'London's lungs' was coined. Two hundred years on they continue to serve as the city's playgrounds, gardens and sportsfields. They have been the setting for events ranging from the Great Exhibition of 1851 to riotous demonstrations.

Londoners fly kites and sail model boats, row dinghies, ride horses, and play football and cricket. They stroll with children and jog for fitness,

Soaking up the sun in Green Park

The Open Air Theatre in Regent's Park

but they do not 'promenade' like southern Europeans. London's parks are informal places where sunbathers strip down to swimsuits, and even pinstriped businessmen remove their jackets and loosen their ties when eating lunch outside in fine weather.

The seasons bring their changes: spring brings a flood of daffodils along Park Lane; in summer, roses perfume the air and band music carries across the grass; autumn means conker-hunting; and in leafless winter, city vistas open up.

Londoners enjoy the parks whatever the weather; cool summer evenings do not deter audiences from the Open Air Theatre in Regent's Park, dog-walkers go out in the rain, and even in winter people wrap up for an energetic stretch of the legs.

The main central parks total some 600 hectares (1,500 acres), but there are countless squares and gardens, churchyards and riverside walks that are also open to the public, and offer a retreat to the city worker, dweller and visitor.

Getting away from it all

Wherever you are in central London, you are never far from a park, a square, a garden or a courtyard that is green and peaceful. The parks can be very busy in good weather, especially during the lunch break on weekdays, but it is usually possible to find a quiet, secluded spot somewhere.

LONDON'S PARKS
Central
Green Park
Green Park is a pleasant haven of lime, plane and hawthorn trees between busy Piccadilly and Constitution Hill.
Tube: Green Park.

Hyde Park
A royal hunting ground for Henry VIII, Hyde Park has been open to the public for some 350 years. It is known for sports ranging from riders on Rotten Row (a corruption of *Route du Roi*) to regular games of softball and touch rugby. You can row a boat on the park's lake, the Serpentine, but only the hardy take a dip on Christmas Day each year. A controversial fountain, dedicated to Princess Diana, was erected in 2004.
Tube: Hyde Park Corner, Marble Arch, Knightsbridge or Lancaster Gate.

Kensington Gardens
Together with Hyde Park, this vast open space totals 249 hectares (615 acres). With the statue of Peter Pan (*see p73*), model boat sailing, and ducks feeding on the pond, this is traditionally the park for children.
Tube: High St Kensington, Queensway or Lancaster Gate.

Regent's Park
The park, as well as the elegant terraces bordering it, was designed by John Nash. Rose-lovers head for Queen Mary's Garden, families for London Zoo and boaters for the lake. Watching summer evening performances in the

HIDDEN CORNERS

Keep your eyes open for secret gardens as they can still be found. In the City, the **courtyard behind St Stephen Walbrook**, with a stringed-bow sundial designed by Henry Moore, is open weekday lunchtimes. **The Conservatory** at the Barbican is a tropical paradise. **Bunhill Fields** on City Road (Old Street tube) is a disused Nonconformist cemetery where three famous writers are buried: John Bunyan, Daniel Defoe and William Blake.

Open Air Theatre can be magical. A panorama of London opens out on Primrose Hill, to the north.
Tube: Regent's Park, Baker St or Great Portland St.

St James's Park
Once the grounds of a leper hospital, this is the oldest of the royal parks. Animals and birds have been kept here since James I's time. The park's natural look, with plane trees and weeping willows, lake and flower beds, is the work of John Nash, the favourite architect of George IV. The park is ideal for a civilised stroll, particularly late afternoon in summer.
Tube: St James's Park.

Further afield
Just out of the city centre are three more open spaces, which are also very popular with Londoners.

Battersea Park
Created for commoners rather than for royalty, this 81-hectare (200-acre) park includes tennis courts, a running track and an old English garden. Spring brings blooms to Cherry Tree and Acacia Avenues and, on the riverside walk, the highlight is a Peace Pagoda, built by Japanese Buddhist monks and nuns in 1985.
Bus: 137 from Sloane Square.

Holland Park
Open to the public since 1952, the former grounds of Holland House have peacocks, the Belvedere Restaurant, a summer theatre and the Kyoto Garden, created for the Japan Festival in 1991. A popular open-air opera season is held every summer.
Tube: Holland Park.

Royal Botanic Gardens, Kew
See p122.

Bridge over the Serpentine, Hyde Park

OTHER GREEN AREAS
Farms
Yes, animals in London, but not in a zoo. There are several successful enterprises now, but **Kentish Town City Farm** was the first, opened in 1972. Its 1.8 hectares (4½ acres) have a real country farmyard feel.
1 Cressfield Close, NW5.
Tel: (020) 7916 5421.
www.ktcityfarm.org.uk. Open: daily 9am–5pm. Free admission.
Tube: Kentish Town or Chalk Farm.

Gardens
The English are a nation of gardeners and, in addition to the public parks, there are many small gardens that are a delight, even if your fingers are not green.

Chelsea Physic Garden
A high brick wall surrounds this fascinating collection of plants established in 1673 by the Society of Apothecaries for medicinal teaching.
66 Royal Hospital Rd, SW3.
Tel: (020) 7352 5646.
www.chelseaphysicgarden.co.uk. Open: Mar–Oct Wed, Thur & Fri noon–5pm, Sun noon–6pm. Admission charge.
Tube: Sloane Square.

Royal Hospital, Chelsea
The gardens next to the river are pleasant for walking dogs, playing tennis or just watching the world go by. Enter by the London or Chelsea Gates; those with dogs, from the Embankment.
Royal Hospital Rd, SW3.
Tel: (020) 7881 5200. www.chelsea-pensioners.co.uk. Open: daily 10am, noon & 2–4pm. Closed: Sun Oct–Mar and all Bank Holidays. Admission charge. Tube: Sloane Square.

London Zoo
See p70.

Regent's Canal
This industrial waterway opened in 1820 to link the Thames with the Grand Union Canal. Boat trips now pass white stucco houses in Little Venice, London Zoo and Regent's Park.
Boat trips: Jason's Trip: Tel: (020) 7286 3428. www.jasons.co.uk. Open: Apr–Nov. Jenny Wren, Canal Cruises:
Tel: (020) 7485 4433.
www.walkersquay.com. Tube: Warwick Ave or Camden Town.

Squares
The Georgians built squares all over central London, and some retain their charm. The shrubbery in St James's Square (SW1) and Russell Square (WC1) creates a garden setting; Soho Square and Golden Square (W1) are havens in bustling Soho; and Fitzroy Square (WC1) is full of blue plaques to artists and authors.

CITY VILLAGES
London is surrounded by villages that have been swallowed up as the metropolis grew. Yet some still retain a strong identity, with plenty of history and greenery, such as these few.

Dulwich

In south London, approximately 8km (5 miles) from the city centre, Dulwich (pronounced Dull-itch) centres on a village with Georgian houses, Victorian cottages and small old-fashioned shops.

Dulwich owes its heritage to Edward Alleyn, a contemporary of Shakespeare, who earned his fortune as an actor and theatre owner. On retiring here in 1612, he built a college, chapel and alms-houses which still stand.

Dulwich Picture Gallery

Britain's first public art gallery was purpose-built by Sir John Soane, who cleverly used natural light to enhance his beautiful building. One of the most popular pictures is Rembrandt's *Girl at a Window*, but there are fine works by Van Dyck, Gainsborough, Watteau and Poussin.
Gallery Rd, SE21. Tel: (020) 8693 5254.
www.dulwichpicturegallery.org.uk.
Open: Tue–Sun 10am–5pm and on all Bank Holiday Mondays. Admission charge. Rail: Victoria to West Dulwich.

Horniman Museum

One of London's most unusual museums, with exotic objects collected from all over the world by the tea importer Frederick Horniman.
100 London Rd, Forest Hill, SE23.
Tel: (020) 8699 1872.
www.horniman.ac.uk.
Open: daily 10.30am–5.30pm. Closed: 24–26 Dec. Gardens: Mon–Sat 7.30am–dusk, Sun 8am–dusk. Free admission. Rail: London Bridge to Forest Hill.

Hampstead

A mere 7km (4¼ miles) north of Piccadilly Circus, hilly Hampstead is a village with an added bonus – 325 hectares (800 acres) of Hampstead Heath on its doorstep. **Kenwood House**, **Fenton House**, **Keats' House** and the **Freud Museum** are all worth a visit, but part of the fun is just exploring Hampstead's lanes and alleys.

Regent's Canal runs through Little Venice

Getting away from it all

Stroll along Heath Street into Church Row with its grand Georgian town houses, window-shop in Flask Walk or wander up to Whitestone Pond on a summer weekend to browse round the arts and crafts market. Drink beer from Young's Brewery at the Flask, Benskins at the Holly Bush, Draught Bass at the Spaniard's Inn and IPA bitter at Jack Straw's Castle, the highest point in London at 135m (440ft) above sea level. *For opening hours see pp62–5.*

Kew

Kew Gardens, officially the Royal Botanic Gardens, has been a scientific research centre for over 200 years, set up with a 'bank' of plants collected during the South Seas voyages of Captain Cook aboard the *Endeavour*.

One of the star attractions is the giant water lily, *Victoria amazonica*, which measures 2m (6½ft) across, in the Princess of Wales Conservatory. This high-tech glasshouse opened in 1987, the year an October hurricane damaged or destroyed nearly 10 per cent of the trees at Kew.

Although the Temperate House is the largest existing Victorian conservatory in the world, and the Alpine House has plants from high altitudes round the globe, it is the Palm House that is the most beautiful. Go up the spiral stairs for a bird's-eye view of a palm forest; downwards leads 'underneath the sea' to Aquaria, which houses marine plants. *Kew. Tel: (020) 8332 5655. www.kew.org. Open: Feb–Mar daily 9.30am–5.30pm; Apr–Aug daily 9.30am–6pm; Oct–Feb 9.30am–4.15pm; glasshouses, museum & gallery close half an hour before the gardens. Admission charge. Tube/rail: Kew Gardens. Rail: Kew Bridge. River boat: Westminster to Kew Pier (summer).*

Richmond

The view from Richmond Hill is impressive. Look down into the Terrace Gardens, then across the Thames Valley, with its water meadows and woods, towards Hampton Court. For centuries, the river was busy with barges, from the luxuriously royal to those laden with fruit and vegetables. Traffic is now on the roads, but this curve of the river remains a delight.

Richmond Park

Charles I commandeered this royal hunting ground in 1635, and surrounded it with a 16km (10-mile) wall.

The largest city park in Europe, here you really are out in the country.

Magnificent Ham House, famed for its extravagant interior

It is home to 600 red and fallow deer, and is ideal for families, who can walk, bicycle and picnic in its 820 hectares (2,026 acres). The rhododendrons and azaleas in the Isabella Plantation are spectacular in late spring.

Riverside Richmond

Only the Tudor gateway remains of Henry VIII's palace, where his daughter Elizabeth I died in 1603. His jousting ground is now a peaceful green, surrounded by Queen Anne and Georgian houses.

Little lanes off the main street and on Richmond Hill are full of interesting shops. Here the towpath becomes a promenade before reverting to a path leading to pretty Petersham village and handsome Ham House.

Ham House

Enter the world of the 17th century in this magnificent country house full of antiques, and amble around the gardens, now restored to the style of their original period. Summer polo matches are played on the adjacent ground.
Ham, Richmond. Tel: (020) 8940 1950. Open: House: mid-Mar–Oct Sat–Wed noon–4pm; Gardens: 11am–6pm. Admission charge for house; garden free. Bus: 65 or 371 from Richmond.

Nearby attractions

Across Kew Bridge, turn right (downstream) for **Strand-on-the-Green**, a delightful collection of riverside houses and pubs. Turn left for two specialist museums on the High Street. The Victorian standpipe tower signposts the **Kew Bridge Steam Museum** where monster engines are steamed up at weekends (*Tel: (020) 8568 4757. www.kbsm.org*). *Open: Tue–Sun 11am–4pm. Admission charge.* The **Musical Museum of Automatic Instruments** is housed in a new lottery-funded building (*Tel: (020) 8560 8108. www.musicalmuseum.co.uk*). *Open: Tue–Sun 11am–5.30pm. Admission charge.*

The Temperate House, Kew Gardens

The Thames

The story of the Thames is the story of London. Think of the Tower of London, the City, the Palace of Westminster – all built on the river. From Hampton Court, Henry VIII's palace southwest of London, to the high-tech Thames Barrier at Woolwich in the east, the Thames twists and turns for 48km (30 miles) past parks and houses, offices and pubs, and beneath a dozen or more bridges. When legs are weary of walking, hop on to what Londoners still call a 'pleasure boat', sit back, and enjoy the unfolding of the London scene.

DOWNSTREAM
Westminster to Waterloo

Opposite Westminster Pier is County Hall, now occupied by a hotel and the London Aquarium. Lining the Victoria bank are the Jubilee Gardens. On the left lie the moored vessels, the *Hispaniola* and *Tattershall Castle*, restaurant and pub. After Hungerford Bridge, the Victoria Embankment Gardens, on the left, front the famous Savoy Hotel; at the riverside stands the ancient Egyptian obelisk, Cleopatra's Needle. On the right is the spectacular London Eye which has dramatically changed the London skyline. Next door is the South Bank Centre, a cultural centre.

Waterloo to Blackfriars

The concrete National Theatre, right, contrasts with the 18th-century elegance of Somerset House on the opposite bank. The latter now houses the Impressionist masterpieces of the Courtauld Institute Galleries. Behind the moored ships *Wellington* and *President* (now offices and entertainment venues) are the gardens of the Temple, where lawyers have their offices. Rising above everything is the dome of St Paul's Cathedral.

Downstream trips run all year round.
Westminster Pier *Tel: (020) 7930 4097.*
To Greenwich, 60 minutes.
To Thames Barrier, 75 minutes.
Embankment Pier
Tel: 0870 781 5049.
To Greenwich, 38 minutes.

Blackfriars to London Bridge

The massive supports of Blackfriars Bridge, shaped like pulpits, recall the monks who once lived on the left bank. On the right, the disused Bankside Power Station has been converted into the exciting Tate Modern art gallery, linked by the Millennium Bridge to the City of London. A narrow house next door is believed to have been used by Christopher Wren during the construction of St Paul's. Experts deny this, but Shakespeare's Globe Theatre was clearly nearby. A reconstruction of the Globe, overlooking the river, opened in 1997.

Past Southwark Bridge and a railway bridge is the modern London Bridge. Its medieval predecessor was a virtual village on the river, and the 19th-century structure was moved stone by stone to a theme park outside Havasu City, Arizona, USA.

London Bridge to Tower Bridge

On the left are two Wren-designed structures: the Monument to the Great Fire of London and, below, St Magnus the Martyr, traditionally the church of fishmongers. Their nearby market, Billingsgate, retains its gilded dolphin weathervane, although the fish merchants moved out in 1981.

Looming on the right is the large HMS *Belfast*, the Tower of London on the left, and Tower Bridge dead ahead.

Tower Bridge to the Thames Barrier

St Katharine Dock on the left and the Design Museum on the right mark the start of Docklands. The old docks have been cleaned up, warehouses restored and pubs rediscovered.

On the left, note the Prospect of Whitby, which has long been known to tourists; it is where Judge Jeffreys, the 17th-century judge who presided over the 'Bloody Assizes', used to drink. He later died in the Tower of London.

The Thames now loops around the Isle of Dogs, which was once one of London's poorest areas and is now dominated by Canary Wharf. At the bottom of the loop lies Greenwich, with the *Cutty Sark* (reopening in spring 2010) and numerous museums, including the **National Maritime Museum**. Wren's Royal Naval College symbolises the city's age-old nautical connection. The river snakes on downstream towards the Thames Barrier, a 20th-century construction (*see p96*).

UPSTREAM
Westminster to Lambeth

The original Westminster Bridge, only the second in central London,

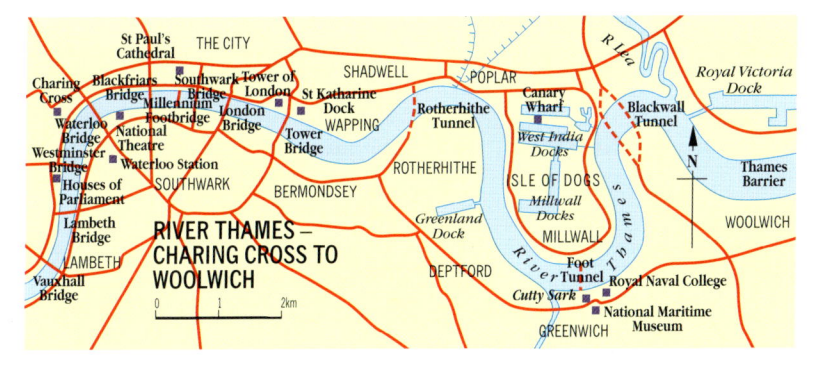

RIVER THAMES – CHARING CROSS TO HAMPTON COURT

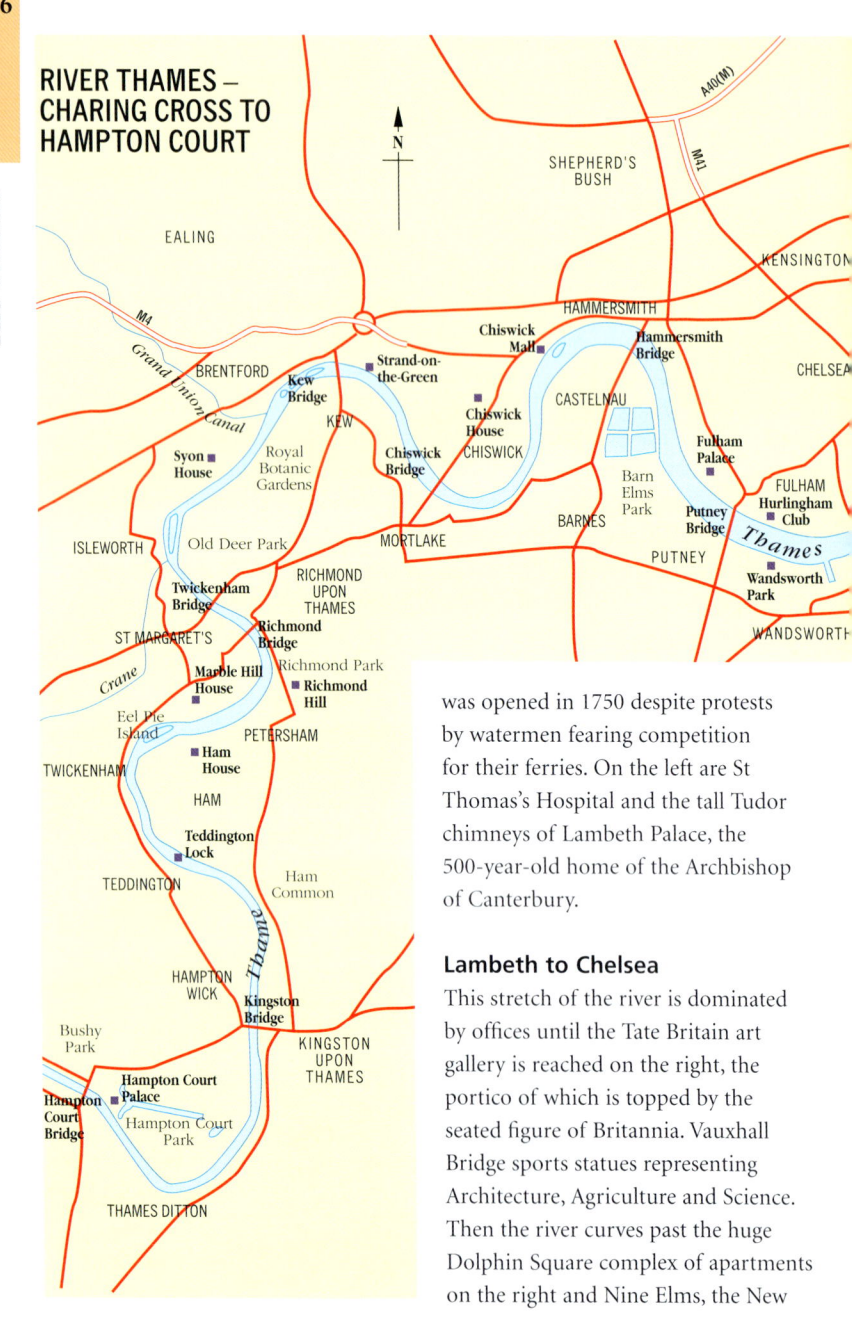

was opened in 1750 despite protests by watermen fearing competition for their ferries. On the left are St Thomas's Hospital and the tall Tudor chimneys of Lambeth Palace, the 500-year-old home of the Archbishop of Canterbury.

Lambeth to Chelsea

This stretch of the river is dominated by offices until the Tate Britain art gallery is reached on the right, the portico of which is topped by the seated figure of Britannia. Vauxhall Bridge sports statues representing Architecture, Agriculture and Science. Then the river curves past the huge Dolphin Square complex of apartments on the right and Nine Elms, the New

Cheyne Walk, which ends at Chelsea Old Church.

Battersea to Putney

Houseboats huddle together on the right bank as the Thames begins a huge loop, passing former warehouses that are being renovated on both sides of the river. The biggest development is Chelsea Harbour on the right, a marina surrounded by flats, restaurants and a hotel. After Wandsworth Bridge, there is greenery on both banks: on the right, the exclusive Hurlingham Club, with croquet lawns and tennis courts; on the left, public Wandsworth Park.
Upstream trips run Easter to October.
Westminster Pier *Tel: (020) 7930 2062.*
To Kew, 1½ hours.
To Richmond, 2 hours.
To Hampton Court, 3½ hours.

Putney to Chiswick

From here westwards the river is increasingly used for sport. Launching

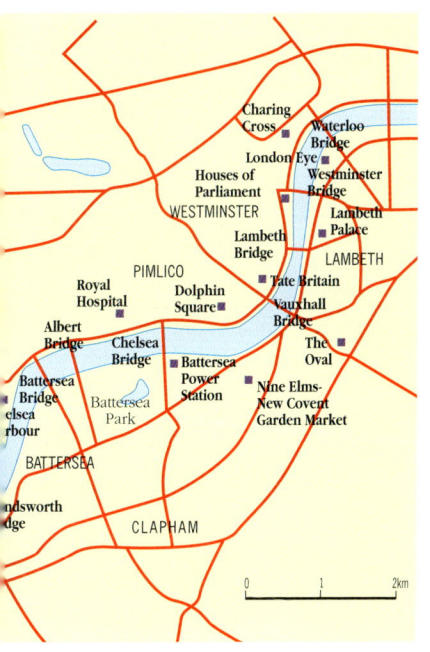

Covent Garden Market, on the left. Unmistakable is the 1930s Battersea Power Station.

Chelsea to Battersea

To the right is the dome of Wren's Royal Hospital for army pensioners. Every May the lawns are covered with tents for the Chelsea Flower Show. On the left are the trees and gardens of Battersea Park, whose riverside walk is punctuated by the gold and white Peace Pagoda, built in 1985 by Buddhist monks and nuns.

Painted in wedding cake colours of rose and pistachio, the Albert Bridge still bears the order for troops to 'break step' when marching across. On the right, the bridge bisects

Sights along the river
Cleopatra's Needle (*see p33*)
Courtauld Institute Galleries (*see p33*)
Docklands (*see pp54–5*)
Greenwich (*see p130*)
The Monument (*see p71*)
Shakespeare's Globe Theatre (*see p104*)
St Paul's (*see pp86–7*)
Somerset House (*see p90*)
South Bank Centre (*see pp92–3*)
Thames Barrier (*see p96*)
Tower Bridge (*see p97*)
Tower of London and environs (*see pp100–3*)
Bards and Bawds walk (*see pp104–5*)

Albert Bridge looks magical at night

ramps and boathouses on the left bank overlook the Universities' stone outside the Star and Garter pub, marking the start of the annual Oxford and Cambridge University Boat Race (usually around Easter). On the right, beyond the grounds of Fulham Palace is Fulham Football Club. Just before Hammersmith, Harrods' huge warehouse sits opposite the Riverside Studios arts centre.

Once under the elegant century-old suspension bridge at Hammersmith, the river begins another loop past Chiswick Mall's elegant Georgian houses. The purpose of the tall posts near the Ship Inn just before Chiswick Bridge is to mark the end of the Boat Race course.

Chiswick to Richmond

Much of London's riverside must once have looked like Strand-on-the-Green, the strip of cottages and pubs on the right bank just before Kew Bridge. Kew Pier on the left is for passengers

MESSING ABOUT ON THE WATER

For centuries, London's waterways represented a means of transport, a source of water and a basic sewage system. The Thames froze regularly during the 18th and 19th centuries. In the summer of 1858, the stench was so foul that curtains soaked in lime had to be draped at the windows of Parliament.

Passengers taking a boat trip upstream to Kew and Hampton Court or downstream to Greenwich may be surprised to see such an abundance of wildlife on the river. Canada geese, herons and cormorants dip and dive among the seagulls to feed off the fish that inhabit the waters.

The Thames is tidal as far as the weir at Teddington, so the level is constantly rising and falling, but now the threat of floods from surge tides is controlled by the Thames Barrier at Woolwich.

wanting to visit the Royal Botanic Gardens at Kew. Once under Kew Bridge, the riverside becomes more rural. On the left are Kew Gardens and Old Deer Park. On the right, look for the lion atop Syon House, part of the Duke of Northumberland's estate.

A lock controls the water flow before Twickenham road and railway bridges. Then, on the left, is the affluent town of Richmond.

Richmond to Hampton Court

Richmond Bridge, built in 1774 and widened in 1939, is the oldest bridge still used on the river. To the left, a steep staircase of houses rises on Richmond Hill. Far below, meadowlands lead to Ham House on the left and Marble Hill House on the right. In the bend is Eel Pie Island, a haunt of rock 'n' rollers back in the 1960s. Then the Thames straightens towards the bridge at Kingston, before majestically sweeping around Hampton Court Park to present a glorious view of the palace. This is how Henry VIII would have seen it, arriving by boat on the River Thames.

Sights along the river
Battersea Park (*see p119*)
Cheyne Walk (*see walk on p34*)
Chiswick Mall (*see walk on p37*)
Kew (*see p122*)
Lambeth Palace (*see p65*)
Richmond (*see pp122–3*)
Royal Hospital, Chelsea (*see walk on p34*)
Tate Britain and Tate Modern (*see pp94–5*)
Westminster and Parliament (*see pp112–13*)

The colourful symmetry of the Tudor Pond Garden, Hampton Court

Excursions

GREENWICH

Greenwich still merits its Saxon name, 'green village', thanks to vast areas of lawns and the huge Greenwich Park. Since Tudor days, however, Greenwich has meant ships. Here, Henry VIII planned the Royal Navy, and Elizabeth I ordered it to repel the Spanish Armada. Greenwich Gateway Visitors' Centre for the World Heritage Site boasts many exhibitions about the history of Greenwich (*open: daily 10am–5pm*).

Cutty Sark

The Concorde of its time, this was the last and fastest of the clipper ships, designed to bring the new season's tea from China to Britain. It is situated in a dry dock. The ship is undergoing a £25 million renovation. However, a fire on the ship in 2007 has delayed the renovation programme and added another £10 million to the bill. The ship hopes to reopen to visitors in summer 2010. Meanwhile, an exhibition centre on site details the restoration project.

National Maritime Museum

Here you can pay homage to heroes like Captain Cook, Sir Francis Drake and other great explorers. One large gallery is devoted to Admiral Lord Nelson.

Old Royal Naval College

Famous for the painted ceiling by Thornhill, this was originally a home for naval pensioners.
Painted Hall & Chapel: Tel: (020) 8269 4747. Open: Mon–Sat 10am–5pm, Sun 12.30–5pm. Free admission. Sun (service 11am).

Old Royal Observatory

This is another Wren building, now a museum, constructed to

Thornhill's painted ceiling at the Old Royal Naval College

accommodate Charles II's interest in astronomy.
National Maritime Museum, Queen's House and Old Royal Observatory. Tel: (020) 8858 4422.
Open: daily 10am–5pm. Free admission. Rail: from Charing Cross or Waterloo East stations. River boat: from Westminster, Charing Cross or Tower Pier.

Queen's House

Designed in 1616 by Inigo Jones for the wife of James I, and completed for the wife of Charles I, the rich interior of this Palladian villa is true to the 17th century. The cantilevered Tulip staircase was the first one built in Britain.

HAMPTON COURT PALACE

From the Lion and Unicorn guarding the entrance, to the King's Beasts at the moat, this looks like a royal castle. It was built by Cardinal Wolsey, but acquired by Henry VIII in 1525. A palace rather than a castle, it has a forest of chimneys rather than fortifications. After Henry VIII the main royal connection is with William and Mary, who in 1689 ordered Christopher Wren to transform the palace into an 'English Versailles'.

The Courtyards

Base Court is Tudor. Note the insignia of Henry and his daughter, Elizabeth I, and also Anne Boleyn's Gateway. Next is Clock Court with the huge Astronomical Clock made in 1540 by the 'Deviser of the King's Horologies'. Fountain Court is 17th-century Wren-designed state and private apartments.

Gardens, Maze and Tennis Courts

The gardens reflect William and Mary's desire for a formal, geometric plan. She was a keen botanist, and included plants from around the world. The famous maze is one of the oldest hedge examples in the country.
Hampton Court Palace, East Molesey. Tel: (0844) 482 7777. www.hrp.org.uk. Open: daily 10am–6pm (4.30pm Nov–Apr). Gardens: daily 7am–6pm. Admission charge. Rail: from Waterloo. River boat: in summer from Westminster Pier.

The Great Hall

In this handsome room (with a hammerbeam roof) costumed performers re-enact the Tudor way of life as Henry VIII's court knew it.

State Apartments

Although little furniture remains except for the royal beds, paintings by Correggio and Titian, together with tapestries and the weapons in the King's Guard Chamber, all combine to form an impressive spectacle.

Tudor Kitchens

The kitchens show preparations for a feast day in 1542. Fifty rooms housed the production line of food for 800 people in winter, and up to 1,200 in summer.

Day trips from London

The destinations listed here are within a couple of hours' travel by train, Green Line bus or National Express coach from Victoria, making for easy and enjoyable days out. Ring the local Tourist Information Centres (TICs) for detailed information and to book accommodation.

BATH

Bath is England's most beautiful Georgian city, but its history goes back much further.

Roman baths

Built on natural hot springs, the Roman temple and baths flourished between the 1st and 5th centuries AD and are remarkably intact. Find them, along with the museum, under the Georgian Pump Room. Take the waters, which smell and taste of rotten eggs!

Georgian city

The 18th-century renaissance of Bath as a spa led to the building of the Circus Terrace, the Royal Crescent and the Assembly Rooms (which today house the fascinating Museum of Costume). The Jane Austen Centre celebrates one of the city's most famous residents. Also visit the Thermae Bath Spa and the American Museum.
Tourist information: Tel: 0906 711 2000.
Rail: from Paddington.

BRIGHTON

The 18th-century craze for sea bathing, together with the Prince Regent's patronage, turned the tiny fishing village of Brighthelmstone into a highly fashionable resort. Surviving stucco elements add elegance, while the Royal Pavilion – Nash's oriental fantasy designed for the Prince – adds eccentricity. All this was overlaid by a layer of now fading Victoriana.

Today, Brighton continues to bustle. The Lanes are prime antique shop browsing territory. The Theatre Royal, the Dome and the more recently built Brighton Centre offer major dramatic, musical and sporting events.
Tourist information: Tel: 0906 711 2255 (50p per minute).
Rail: from Victoria.

CAMBRIDGE

Situated on the banks of the River Cam, this beautiful city is completely dominated by its historic university, which dates back to the 13th century.

The colleges

There are 31 colleges, all within easy walking distance of each other. It is a pleasure to wander around the chapels and courtyards and in the college gardens that stretch back to the river. Follow the course of the waterway – either in a punt or by foot over the succession of picturesque bridges.

Magnificent King's College Chapel is famed for its fan-vaulting and stained-glass windows. Trinity, founded by Henry VIII, is noted for its Great Court; St John's for its Venetian-inspired Bridge of Sighs; Pembroke for its Wren chapel. Also visit the Fitzwilliam Museum and the tower of Great St Mary's for a view of the city.
Tourist information: Tel: (01223) 464732. Rail: from King's Cross or Liverpool St.

CANTERBURY

Built on seven islands in the River Stour, the city is a delight to discover on foot. Start with a 'timewalk' through history from Roman times to World War II at the Canterbury Museum on the riverbank.

The cathedral

Best known as the site of Archbishop Thomas à Becket's martyrdom, the cathedral has long been a pilgrimage centre as well as the focal point for world-wide Anglicanism. It is noted for its stained glass, Norman crypt and the tomb of the Black Prince. Also visit The Canterbury Tales.
Tourist information: Tel: (01227) 378100. Rail: from Victoria or Charing Cross.

Day trips from London

A punt glides by the west end of King's College Chapel, Cambridge

DOVER

The busiest ferry port in Europe is just a transit point for millions passing to and from France. Yet Dover, the gateway to England, has its own place in history.

White Cliffs

The chalk ridge of the North Downs meets the sea in spectacular fashion. The National Trust runs a visitors' centre and café.

The castle

Known as the Key of England, the imposing castle stands right on top of the White Cliffs, an important strategic site from the Iron Age to World War II. The keep rivals the White Tower at the Tower of London in grandeur. Hellfire Corner refers to the network of early 19th-century tunnels where the World War II evacuation from Dunkirk was masterminded.
Tourist information: Tel: (01304) 205108.
Rail: from Victoria or Charing Cross.

HEVER CASTLE

Dating from the 13th century, this is where Henry VIII courted his second wife, Anne Boleyn. Early last century, William Waldorf Astor added the Tudor village, the lake and the magnificent gardens.
Hever Castle and Gardens, Hever, near Edenbridge, Kent.
Tel: (01732) 865224.
www.hevercastle.co.uk.
Rail: from Victoria (to Edenbridge).

LEEDS CASTLE

This moated fortification lives up to its claim of being 'the loveliest castle in the world'. Excellent grounds include a duckery, a maze-grotto, woodlands, the Culpeper Garden and the aviary.
Maidstone, Kent. Tel: (01622) 765400.
www.leeds-castle.com.
Rail: from Victoria (to Bearsted), then connecting coach – combined ticket for travel and entrance available from Victoria Station or National Express.

LINCOLN

This small, hilltop city is off the tourist trail. As well as the ancient cathedral and castle, there is the Roman Newport Arch, still used by traffic, and Steep Hill with its shops.

The cathedral

Dominating the entire city is the massive 900-year-old, triple-towered cathedral at the top of Steep Hill. Inside, look for the famous carving of the 'Lincoln Imp'.

The castle

In 1068 William the Conqueror ordered 166 Saxon dwellings to be demolished in order to build his castle opposite the cathedral. Fine views extend from the ramparts, but the coffin-like box pews of the Victorian Prison Chapel recall the hard lives of convicts. Also visit the Usher Art Gallery, the Museum of Lincolnshire Life and the National Cycle Museum.

Tourist information: Tel: (01522) 526450. Rail: from King's Cross (change at Newark).

OXFORD

The name is known worldwide but the university, with its 39 colleges, is only part of this thriving city.

Confederation of Colleges

Sixteenth-century Christ Church Chapel – Oxford Cathedral – contains windows by William Morris and Burne-Jones. Walk along the river in Christ Church Meadows to the Botanic Gardens, then into Magdalen, possibly the most beautiful of the colleges. Exeter College has a unique 17th-century dining room, and Merton a medieval library.

The Ashmolean Museum houses a noted collection of European paintings as well as prints, coins and ceramics. The old covered market in the city centre still bustles with stalls and shops.
Tourist information: Tel: (01865) 252200. Rail: from Paddington.

Blenheim Palace

This ornate 18th-century palace was the gift of Queen Anne to the 1st Duke of Marlborough in recognition of his great victory over the French at Blenheim, Bavaria. There are splendid furnishings inside. Outside are parklands designed by 'Capability' Brown.
Blenheim Palace, Woodstock, Oxon.
Tel: (0870) 060 2080.
www.blenheimpalace.com.
Rail: Paddington to Oxford, then bus.

STONEHENGE AND SALISBURY

Stonehenge is awe-inspiring. The circle of stones set in the vast Salisbury Plain dates from 2800 BC to 1400 BC, and was built in roughly three stages by late Neolithic and Bronze Age peoples. But how and why were they brought

The ancient circle of standing stones at Stonehenge

here? Most agree that Stonehenge was a place of worship, with ceremonies marking the seasons, especially the summer solstice. Decide for yourself how these stones were transported all the way from Wales – before the wheel was invented!

Salisbury

The cathedral, built between 1220 and 1258, has a unity of style unusual in medieval cathedrals. Its spire, the highest in England, was a 14th-century addition and can be seen for miles around. In the Chapter House is an original copy of Magna Carta; outside, the Cathedral Close contains examples of architecture from the 13th century to the present day.
Tourist information: Tel: (01722) 434373. Rail: from Waterloo.

STRATFORD-UPON-AVON

On the 'must-see' list of every first-time visitor to Britain, this old market town retains a charm despite being swamped by coach-loads of tourists. Take a rowing boat or a punt to enjoy the River Avon and the beautiful surrounding countryside.

The Shakespeare Trail

Shakespeare's birthplace, a half-timbered house, has been furnished to retain its original middle-class appearance and includes an exhibition of his life and work.

Other sights in town (worth buying an inclusive ticket) are: New Place, Shakespeare's retirement home; Hall's Croft, where his married daughter lived; and Anne Hathaway's Cottage, the thatched family home of his wife.

Winchester Cathedral in leafy Hampshire

The Royal Shakespeare Company
The season of plays at the RSC's three theatres runs from November to August/September. Enthusiasts should take the Theatre Tour and see the RSC exhibition of costumes, props, photographs and other memorabilia.
Tourist information: Tel: (0870) 160 7930. RSC information: Tel: (01789) 403444. Rail: from Paddington.

WINCHESTER
Once a Roman city, this became the capital of England under Alfred the Great. The Great Hall is the only visible reminder of the Norman castle later rebuilt by Henry III. A massive round table hangs on the wall, carved with the names of King Arthur and his knights.

The cathedral
Unprepossessing outside but fascinating inside, this building was started soon after the Norman Conquest. It is the longest of any medieval cathedral in Europe. The tomb of Jane Austen is here.
Tourist information: Tel: (01962) 840500. Rail: Waterloo.

WINDSOR
The castle
This towered and turreted complex is the oldest and largest inhabited castle in the world. From its hilltop position 40km (25 miles) west of London), it overlooks the cobbled streets of the town, Eton College, the River Thames and Home Park. William the

The crenellations of Windsor Castle are prominent on the skyline

Conqueror chose the site for a fortress, but what we see dates from the time of Henry II (12th century) and later kings. Ten monarchs are buried in St George's Chapel, and the State Apartments are worth seeing. Windsor was also the location of Prince Charles's second marriage to Camilla Parker-Bowles in April 2005.
Tourist information: Tel: (01753) 743900. Rail: from Paddington (change at Slough) to Windsor & Eton Central, or Waterloo to Windsor & Eton Riverside.

Legoland Windsor
A theme park 3km (1³/₄ miles) from Windsor featuring scale models of buildings, trains, cars, ships and people made from millions of Lego bricks. 'Miniland' recreates scenes from major European cities. There are also interactive rides and attractions.
Legoland Windsor, Winkfield Rd. Tel: (0871) 2222 001. Rail as above, then shuttle bus from Windsor.

Shopping

There are good stores all over London. For an extensive guide to shops and markets in London, get Time Out London's Shops & Services Guide, *available at bookshops and good newsagents. Given below is a very general list of the main shopping areas.*

GOOD SHOPPING AREAS
The West End (W1)

Oxford Street claims to be the longest shopping street in Europe. It is usually crowded with serious shoppers going in and out of well-known chain stores and department stores.

Just off Oxford Street (near Bond Street tube station) are two pedestrian precincts lined with upmarket shops, selling mainly fashion and accessories. To the south is **South Molton Street**, to the north **St Christopher's Place**.

Regent Street is a gracious curve running from Oxford Circus to Piccadilly Circus. At the top end is Liberty (department store) and Hamleys (toys), with Aquascutum and Austin Reed (fashion) towards the bottom. In between are Mappin & Webb (silver) and Waterford Wedgwood (glass, china).

Piccadilly boasts Waterstones, Hatchards (books) and Fortnum & Mason (food and accessories).

Just south of Piccadilly is **Jermyn Street**, with old-fashioned-looking shops, some dating back centuries, and stocked with high-quality ladies' and gentlemen's clothing and accessories. (*See* Walk, p84.)

Linking Piccadilly and Oxford Street is **Bond Street**. It is divided into the old southern and new northern end. This has some of the most expensive shops in the city, from designer clothes to gifts at Asprey and Tiffany & Co, respectively.

ARCADES

America's indoor shopping malls were pre-dated by London's arcades like the Burlington Arcade, off Piccadilly, W1. Doormen in livery add to the Regency atmosphere of upmarket boutiques selling cashmere and antique jewellery.

The Royal Arcade off Bond Street and the Piccadilly and Prince's arcades on the south of Piccadilly are similar. (Tube: Green Park or Piccadilly Circus.)

A modern version of the arcades is Whiteley's, once a staid department store, now full of shops, restaurants and cinemas. (Tube: Queensway.)

Knightsbridge and Chelsea

Knightsbridge and **Brompton Road**, SW1, have Harrods and Harvey Nichols department stores as the mainstays, but there are other shops, like The Scotch House and Jaeger (clothes).

Sloane Street, SW1, provides a continuation of upmarket shopping from Knightsbridge to **Sloane Square**, where the General Trading Company (where posh couples have their wedding lists) and Peter Jones department store can fill most needs. From Sloane Square, the **King's Road**, Chelsea, SW3, bustles with shops, antique markets, fashionable boutiques and wine bars.

From Knightsbridge tube station, Brompton Road leads to **Beauchamp Place** (pronounced Bee-chum), full of small boutiques, restaurants and designer fashion outlets. Further along is another fashionable area: **Walton Street** and **'Brompton Cross'**, with the trendy Joseph store and the art deco Michelin Building housing Sir Terence Conran's designer shop and restaurants at its core.

Kensington High Street, W8, is lively, with plenty of chain stores and individual shops. **Kensington Church Street**, known for its antique shops, is also worth a look.

Shops in London are open all day, six days a week (but most now also open Sundays), with late-night shopping until 7pm on Wednesday in Knightsbridge, and until 8pm on Thursday on Oxford Street. The main sales are in January and July.

VAT (Value Added Tax), a European Union sales tax, can be reimbursed to visitors from outside the EU.

The Burlington Arcade first opened in 1819

Liberty department store was founded in 1875

WHAT TO BUY
Antiques
Dealers
It is impossible to list them all, but the best seem to have congregated in Kensington Church Street, W8; Bond Street, W1; Camden Passage, N1; Portobello Road, and Westbourne Grove, W11. Stalls in indoor 'markets' also sell bric-à-brac.

Alfie's
13–25 Church St, NW8. Open: Tue–Sat 10am–6pm. Tube: Edgware Rd.

Antiquarius
131–141 King's Rd, SW3. Open: Mon–Sat 10am–6pm. Tube: Sloane Square.

Chenil Galleries
181–183 King's Rd, SW3. Open: Mon–Sat 10am–6pm. Tube: Sloane Square.

Gray's Antiques Market
58 Davies St & 1–7 Davies Mews, W1. Open: Mon–Fri 10am–6pm. Tube: Bond St.

Books
New
After 300 years at 187 Piccadilly, Hatchards must be doing something right! The legendary Foyles is on Charing Cross Road, one of the world's largest bookshops. Waterstones, also on Piccadilly, is very comprehensive, too.

Second-hand
Charing Cross Road is the place for reasonably priced and bargain bookshops, and Cecil Court for speciality, antiquarian and many first-edition books.

China and glass
Waterford Wedgwood combine the best of both worlds – Irish crystal and English bone china – at their stores in Regent Street and Piccadilly. Peter Jones at Sloane Square has a good range and competitive prices.

Electronics
Tottenham Court Road is lined with cheap specialist shops selling the latest video cameras, televisions and electronic games.

Fabrics
Material for men's suits can be bought by the metre from shops like J & J Minnis. Women enjoy the huge range at John Lewis (Oxford Street) and nearby Liberty (Regent Street) with its famous prints.

Jewellery
Hatton Garden has been the centre of the jewellery trade since medieval times. Garrard (New Bond Street) is an incarnation of another era. Go to Electrum Gallery on South Molton Street for contemporary jewellery.

Lingerie
The fashion for feminine, sexy-with-style undergarments was started by British designer Janet Reger. Check out Agent Provocateur at Broadwick Street in Soho.

Music
Several giant stores stock a wide range of CDs, cassettes, records (to a lesser extent) and videos – HMV is the best known.

Perfume and toiletries
Part of the English tradition and worth visiting for sensual pleasure alone are Floris on Jermyn Street and Penhaligon's on Wellington Street, Covent Garden.

Shoes
Chains like Russell and Bromley and Jones are reliable. John Lobb (St James's Street) and Trickers (Jermyn Street) are the made-to-measure specialists for men. Women who can afford it go to Manolo Blahnik in Chelsea.

Silver
The London Silver Vaults (off Chancery Lane) are an Aladdin's cave of dealers with old and modern silver (*see p70*). Garrard on Albemarle Street and Mappin & Webb on Regent Street are traditional shops.

Sports equipment
JD Sports stores, especially 268–269 Oxford Street, are exciting to visit. Lillywhite's at Piccadilly Circus could equip several Olympic teams.

Toys and games
Hamleys of Regent Street is among the biggest toy shops in the world; Disney is on Oxford Street, but model fanatics head for Beatties in Holborn.

Woollens and knitwear
One of the best buys in London and available in hundreds of stores. Marks & Spencer and Burberry are particularly good.

Regent Street is lined with expensive shops

Quality china is on sale at Thomas Goode

WHERE TO BUY

Burberry for raincoats.
21–23 New Bond Street, W1S, & branches.

Charbonnel et Walker for theatre boxes of 'non-rustle' chocolates.
28 Old Bond St, W1.

Ede & Ravenscroft for robes, wigs and waistcoats.
93 Chancery Lane, WC2.

Farlow's for fishing tackle.
9 Pall Mall, SW1.

Floris for traditional English perfumes.
89 Jermyn St, W1.

W & H Gidden for saddles and custom-made leather goods.
15d Clifford St, W1.

Thomas Goode for luxury china and glass.
19 South Audley St, W1.

DR Harris for their 'pick-me-up' hangover cure.
29 St James's St, W1.

Holland & Holland for hunting rifles and shotguns.
33 Bruton St, W1.

Jaeger for stylish woollen clothing.
200 Regent St, W1, & branches.

Jo Malone for soaps.
150 Sloane St, SW1, & branches.

Laura Ashley for English country-look clothes, fabrics and home furnishings.
House of Fraser, 318 Oxford St, W1.

Lobb for men's shoes.
9 St James's St, SW1.

James Lock & Co for bowler hats (called 'cokes').
6 St James's St, SW1.

Moyses Flowers for flowers.
16 Motcomb St, SW1.

Pringle of Scotland for knitwear.
112 New Bond St, W1.

Turnbull & Asser for made-to-measure shirts.
71–72 Jermyn St, W1.

Markets

London still has a surprisingly large number of thriving stall holders, happy to shout out the day's bargains – from apples to antiques. Non-trade shoppers can visit the farmers' markets held at weekends. Most of these open early and start to close by early afternoon. Arrive early to avoid disappointment!

Bermondsey (New

Bargains can still be found …

Cheerful Berwick Street Market in the heart of Soho has a wide range of fruit and vegetables

Caledonian Market). Go here on Fridays only, and early, for bric-à-brac and antiques. *SE1. Tube: London Bridge.*

Borough Market
A must for 'foodies'. *Open: Thur–Sat. SE1. Tube: London Bridge.*

Brixton
Mainly household goods, food and some second-hand stalls, all with a flavour of the Caribbean. Best on a Saturday. *SW9. Open: Mon–Sat (closed: Wed afternoon). Tube: Brixton.*

Camden Lock
Crafts and bric-à-brac to appeal to the young, trendy and alternative. *NW1. Open: daily. Tube: Camden Town.*

Columbia Road Market
Trendy market in the East End for all things 'floral'. Soak up the atmosphere with a frothy cup of coffee! *E2. Open: Sunday mornings. Tube: Old St/ Bethnal Green.*

Covent Garden Jubilee Market
Good quality, few bargains. Monday for antiques, otherwise mainly crafts. *WC2. Tube: Covent Garden.*

Petticoat Lane
Actually a section of Middlesex St, the market spills into Cobb, Wentworth and Goulston Streets. Fruit, vegetables and household goods. During the week the market is at Wentworth Street, expanding into other streets on Sundays. *E1. Open: Sun–Fri 9am– 2pm. Tube: Aldgate, Aldgate East or Liverpool St.*

Portobello Road
The most famous of all. Originally just a Saturday antique market, it has expanded over the years into nearby streets. Stalls throughout the week sell household goods, bric-à-brac and second-hand clothes. Best at weekends. *W11. Open: Mon–Sat. Tube: Notting Hill Gate or Ladbroke Grove.*

... if you know what you're looking for

Shopper's Eden

Britain was called a 'nation of shopkeepers' by Napoleon, and London is the capital of shopping. Many of its stores are tourist attractions in their own right. Harrods appeals to shoppers and non-shoppers alike; Liberty of Regent Street has thousands of metres of beautiful fabrics; and where else for raincoats but Aquascutum and Burberry? Londoners shop in speciality stores that sell everything from antiques, books and cartoons, to toys, walking sticks and zithers; or in huge department stores like Selfridges, John Lewis and Debenhams. They can browse in cheap and cheerful outdoor markets, or enjoy formal service at Fortnum & Mason and old-fashioned shops in Jermyn Street. They can mix with the crowds along Oxford Street, or head for new enclaves like Brompton Cross in South Kensington. They can shop under cover in 18th-century malls like Burlington Arcade, or the converted Whiteley's complex of shops, cinemas and cafés in Bayswater.

Ever since 'throwaway fashion' became trendy in the 1960s, London has been a great place for buying the latest look at affordable

Strolling past Prada on Bond Street

prices. Well-made British classics such as sweaters and tweeds can be found throughout the West End and are bought by Londoners as well as by visitors.

Souvenirs can range from tacky T-shirts and hats to handmade shoes, but do not forget museum shops. They are excellent hunting grounds for the unusual: copies of ancient jewellery at the British Museum, or the latest in modern craftsmanship at the Victoria & Albert.

Whatever Londoners, or visitors, want to buy, they will be able to find it, somewhere.

A shopping trip souvenir

Liberty's Tudor Revival façade

Entertainment

Many cities claim to be entertainment capitals, but none can compete with the wide range of live and recorded artistic performances available day in, day out in London. There are nightclubs to suit all tastes and a choice of casinos for those who still have money to spend.

London's theatre is justly regarded as the best in the world, whether it is a Shakespeare tragedy, an Alan Ayckbourn comedy, an Andrew Lloyd Webber musical, or a typically British farce by Ray Cooney. Actors and actresses who are familiar on television and film are still prepared to put their reputations on the line, live on the West End stage. No wonder more than 12 million tickets are sold annually in over 50 major theatres, let alone the enterprising 'fringe' theatres and pubs. Theatre is an

You may be entertained while queuing for tickets at Covent Garden

THEATRE TICKETS

A few golden rules for buying tickets.
1. Buy direct from the theatre – there is no service charge; telephone bookings with a credit card may incur a charge.
2. You can also call a registered ticket agency: **Keith Prowse** (*Tel: 0870 840 1111*) or **Ticketmaster** (*Tel: 0870 4000 700*). Credit cards incur a hefty surcharge. Check exactly how much.
3. Matinées are often less crowded and slightly cheaper than evening performances.
4. The Tkts Booth in Leicester Square sells good seats at half-price. Line up from noon for matinée and evening shows but expect up to an hour's wait (there is no telephone line for enquiries).
5. Students and senior citizens get standby tickets to matinée and evening shows.
6. Never risk your money buying tickets from street 'touts'. The price will be inflated and the ticket may be fake. Also avoid the indoor touts at small shops or stalls looking like ticket agencies.

informal night out for many people, content to pop into a show at the last minute, as well as booking ahead for the popular blockbuster shows.

London has no fewer than five orchestras, and unlike many European cities, there is no summer break, so you can enjoy good music with great soloists and conductors at any time of year.

Although opera and ballet are the most expensive entertainments, standards are high, and glamorous, glittering evenings are often graced by royalty. On the popular front, London was the birthplace of rock groups like the Rolling Stones, the Who and Queen, all of whom graduated from the 'local' pubs and clubs which are still the stepping stones to recording success.

Although London still has a reputation for closing down at midnight as pubs and public transport (except for a night bus service) grind to a halt, plenty of clubs and restaurants keep the party going to the small hours to test the stamina of the most avid dancers and merrymakers.

Cinema

First-run films are shown at the big West End cinemas, all in the area around Piccadilly Circus.

The busy **British Film Institute** on the South Bank has a constantly changing array of films, often themed round a country, a director, or a particular genre.
South Bank, SE1.
Tel: (020) 7928 3232.
www.bfi.org.uk.
Tube: Waterloo.

A performance at Shakespeare's Globe Theatre

Classical music

The Barbican Centre is home to the London Symphony Orchestra.
Tel: (020) 7638 4141.
www.barbican.org.uk.
Tube: Moorgate or Barbican.

The Royal Albert Hall is a fine, old-fashioned setting, modernised with mushroom-like acoustic panels in the domed ceiling. The Henry Wood Promenade Concerts (the 'Proms') in July, August and September are a highlight of the British music scene – some 70 concerts are played in 50 days, with inexpensive tickets for the 'promenaders', who stand.
Tel: (020) 7589 8212.
www.royalalberthall.com.
Tube: High St Kensington or Knightsbridge.

The South Bank Centre has three concert halls: the large Royal Festival Hall, home of the London Philharmonic Orchestra; the smaller Queen Elizabeth Hall, where the Opera Factory performs; and the Purcell Room.
Tel: 0871 663 2501.
www.southbankcentre. org.uk.
Tube: Waterloo or Embankment.

The small **Wigmore Hall** with its excellent acoustics is a perfect setting for chamber groups and soloists.
36 Wigmore St.
Tel: (020) 7258 8200.
Tube: Oxford Circus or Bond St.

Dance

The Royal Opera House is also the home of the prestigious Royal Ballet, while Sadler's Wells hosts dance companies from around the world throughout the year.

Jazz

Although Ronnie Scott's club has become an institution after 25 years in Soho, there are others.
Pizza Express Jazz Club
10 Dean St, W1.
Tel: 0845 6027 017. Tube: Tottenham Court Rd.
Pizza on the Park
11 Knightsbridge, SW1.
Tel: (020) 7235 7825.
Tube: Hyde Park Corner.
Ronnie Scott's
47 Frith St, W1.
Tel: (020) 7439 0747.
Tube: Piccadilly Circus.

Opera and ballet

The London Coliseum is where the English National Opera performs in English.
Tel: (020) 7836 0111.
www.eno.org. Tube: Charing Cross or Leicester Square.

The Royal Opera House, usually referred to as 'Covent Garden', is where stars like Carlos Acosta and Placido Domingo regularly perform.
Tel: (020) 7304 4000.
www.roh.org.uk.
Tube: Covent Garden.

Rock and pop

All the world's superstars arrive in London at some point on their tours, usually playing at big indoor venues. Weekly *Time Out* magazine gives concert listings.
Carling Apollo Hammersmith
Tel: 0870 771 2000.
Tube: Hammersmith & Shepherd's Bush.
Wembley Arena
Tel: (020) 8762 5500.
Tube: Wembley Park.

Theatre

The National Theatre Company plays in the

Lyttelton, Olivier and Cottesloe theatres.
Tel: (020) 7452 3000.
Tube: Waterloo.
The **West End** is also the home of commercial theatre as opposed to the above state-supported company. Most of the famous theatres are within 10 minutes' walk of Piccadilly Circus.

Theatre tours
Some theatres offer backstage tours.
The National Theatre
Tel: (020) 7452 3000.
Theatre Royal, Drury Lane
Tel: 0870 890 6002.

LATE-NIGHT LONDON
Not so long ago, London was known as a city that closed at 11pm. Now, more clubs open at 11pm and blast out music until the early hours, even up to 6am. The law that prevented drinking establishments from opening past 11pm was recently revoked, and London is now like any other late-night city. 'One nighters' are

Rock as well as classical music can be heard at the Royal Albert Hall

Leicester Square has always been an entertainment area

popular. This is when a DJ takes over a club for the night, attracting clubbers to his style of music. The music can range from zouk and soca to balearic and zydeco. *Time Out* magazine has weekly club listings.

Casinos

The gambling boom of the 1970s has subsided, but there are still many casinos happy to take your money. Small casinos like the **Ritz**, **Crockfords** and **Aspinalls** require sponsors for new members, but the **London Park Tower** is unrestricted. *101 Knightsbridge, SW1. Tel: (020) 7235 6161. Tube: Knightsbridge.*

Comedy/cabaret

London now leads the world in comedy with clubs like the **Comedy Store** (*1A Oxendon St, SW1. Tel: 0844 847 1728*) and **Jongleurs** (*49 Lavender Gardens, SW11. Tel: 0207 228 3744*). Stand-up comedians will shock as well as amuse with their 'alternative' or 'new' comedy. **Madame Jo Jo's** is London's best cabaret/drag show (*8–10 Brewer St, W1. Tel: (020) 7734 3040). Tube: Piccadilly Circus.*

Lesbian and gay

Listed below are two of the established clubs on the lesbian and gay scene. Phone the London Lesbian & Gay Switchboard for more details: *Tel: (020) 7837 7324* (24 hours), or check *Time Out* magazine.

Heaven
Under the Arches, Villiers St, WC2. Tel: (020) 7930 2020. Tube: Embankment or Charing Cross.

G-A-Y Bar
30 Old Compton St, W1. Tel: (020) 7494 2756. Tube: Leicester Square.

Nightclubs

London has a lively music scene and is

FREE

The foyers of the bigger complexes like the Barbican and South Bank often have free live entertainment at lunchtime and early evenings. In the summer, the street entertainers in Covent Garden Piazza continue into the evening.

blessed with a large number of nightclubs. Two of Europe's biggest are in the West End.

Electric Ballroom
184 Camden High St, NW1. Tel: (020) 7485 9006. Tube: Camden Town.

Fabric
77A Charterhouse St, EC1. Tel: (020) 7336 8898. Tube: Farringdon.

Matter
O2, Peninsula Square, SE10. Tel: (020) 7549 6686. Tube: Greenwich.

Ministry of Sound
103 Gaunt St, SE1. Tel: 0844 499 3456. Tube: Elephant & Castle.

Notting Hill Arts Club
21 Notting Hill Gate, W11. Tel: (020) 7460 4459. Tube: Notting Hill.

Salsa
96 Charing Cross Rd, WC2. Tel: (020) 7379 3277. Tube: Leicester Square.

More sophisticated is:
Café de Paris
Famous since 1926.
3 Coventry St, W1.
Tel: (020) 7734 7700. Tube: Leicester Square.

Pub music

One of the best ways to find out how ordinary Londoners enjoy life is to go to a pub when it is hosting a band. The Half Moon at Putney and the Lonsdale at Notting Hill are just a few, but there are dozens of lively spots to spend the evening. Again, *Time Out* magazine has details. *www.timeout.com/london*

You can find a gig or club every night of the week

Children

'Children should be seen but not heard' was the Victorian attitude to little ones. Nowadays, as well as parks and gardens, London's museums and galleries hum with the sound of happy children eager to learn from the interactive computer and video technology. Trails and quizzes add to the fun. Ask what's on offer specifically for children wherever you go. For example, the Cabinet War Rooms have a special audio tape designed for children, quite different from the adult version.

In addition to the main listings, the following are particularly enjoyable for youngsters. It is also worth looking at the children's listing in *Time Out* magazine for children's activities around the city. Many attractions in London offer discounts for children.

Babysitters
To give parents a break!
Universal Aunts
Tel: (020) 7738 8937.

Battersea Park Children's Zoo
A zoo perfect for children of any age. It includes flamingoes, otters, deer and monkeys among other animals.
Battersea Park, SW11. Tel: (020) 7924 5826. www.batterseaparkzoo.co.uk. Open: daily 10am–5.30pm (4pm in winter). Admission charge. Rail: Battersea Park.

Horniman Museum
A family-friendly museum of natural history and anthropology

DID YOU SEE?
The light in Big Ben's clock tower? It means the House of Commons is in session.
The Royal Standard (flag) on Buckingham Palace? If so, the Queen is in residence.

with a new, modernised aquarium.
100 London Rd, SE23. Open: daily 10.30am–5.30pm. Closed: 24–26 Dec. Rail: Forest Hill.

Ice rinks
The Natural History Museum, Somerset House and the Tower of London all have outdoor ice rinks during the winter months. There is also a small rink at Broadgate.
Broadgate
Eldon St, EC2. Tel: (020) 7505 4068. Open: Nov–early Apr daily. Admission charge. Tube: Liverpool St.
Natural History Museum
Exhibition Rd, SW7.
Tel: 0844 847 1576. Open: early Nov–mid-Jan daily. Admission charge. Tube: South Kensington.

Broadgate Ice Rink provides an exercise space in the City

Somerset House
The Strand, WC2. Tel: (020) 7845 4600.
Open: from late Nov–end Jan daily.
Admission charge.
Tube: Temple (not on Sun),
Covent Garden or Holborn.

Tower of London
Tower Hill, EC3. Tel: 0844 412 4640.
Open: late Nov–mid-Jan daily.
Admission charge.
Tube: Tower Hill.

DID YOU KNOW?

You can sign the Queen's Visitors' Book – ask the policeman at the main entrance of Buckingham Palace.

You can make a brass rubbing of a king or queen at Westminster Abbey or a medieval knight at St Martin-in-the-Fields. Wax and paper are provided at their Brass Rubbing Centres.

London Aquarium
Scores of brilliantly coloured fish and an impressive shark tank.
The County Hall, Riverside Bldg, SE1.
Tel: (020) 7967 8000.
www.londonaquarium.co.uk.
Open: daily 10am–6pm.
Admission charge.
Tube: Waterloo.

London Eye
See p23.

London Zoo
See p70.

Open-top bus tours
Ride in an open-top bus round the sights, all with live guides plus recorded commentary in eight languages.

Friendly rays at the London Aquarium

Big Bus Tours
24-hour tickets are on sale on the buses or online. Join a tour at any bus stop. There are two tours: Big Ben, Buckingham Palace and Madame Tussaud's or Trafalgar Square, St Paul's Cathedral and Tower of London.
48 Buckingham Palace Rd, SW1.
Tel: (020) 7233 9533.
www.bigbustours.com.
Tours start 8.30am, last tours start 4.30pm Nov–Feb, 6pm Apr–Sept.

Outdoor fun
When children (and parents) cannot face another museum or indoor amusement, head for something different (summer or winter) to work off surplus energy. Look in the **Getting Away From it All** section for parks, canal trips and the City Farm (*p120*), or try the following:

Boat trips and canal trips
See pp124–9 and p32.

Changing of the Guard
Every child (and adult!) should see this at least once. Get there early to ensure a good position.
Buckingham Palace, SW1. Occurs daily in summer, alternate days in winter: 11.30am. (See also p28.)

Coram Fields
A children's playground with sports facilities, pets' corner, and other animals in the centre of London.

93 Guilford St, WC1.
Tel: (020) 7837 6138.
www.coramsfields.org.
Open: daily 9am–7pm, until dusk in winter.
Closed: 25–26 Dec. Free admission.
Tube: Russell Square.

Riding

Riding a horse along Hyde Park's Rotten Row is an exhilarating experience.
Ross Nye Riding Stables, 8 Bathurst Mews, W2.
Tel: (020) 7262 3791. Open: daily (except Mon). Reservation essential.
Tube: Lancaster Gate.

Rowing

You can hire boats on the lakes in Regent's Park and on the Serpentine in Hyde Park.

Theatres

Many musicals in the West End are suitable for younger children.

Little Angel Theatre
Tel: (020) 7226 1787.
Mirage Children's Theatre
Tel: (020) 7349 9969.
Polka Theatre for Children
Tel: (020) 8543 4888.
Puppet Theatre Barge
Tel: (020) 7249 6876.
Unicorn Theatre for Children
Tel: (020) 7645 0560.

Eating out

There are plenty of fast-food burger and pizza outlets to keep children happy.

Most children love the Chinese restaurants in Soho's Chinatown. (*See* Food and Drink, *pp164–9, for listings.*)

V & A Museum of Childhood attracts adults as well as children

Crumpet
A tea and crumpets child-friendly café.
66 Northcote Rd, SW11.
Tel: (020) 7924 1117. www.crumpet.biz.
Open: Mon–Sat 9am–6pm, Sun 10am–6pm.

La Famiglia
Italian, family-orientated and serves authentic dishes.
7 Langton St, SW10. Tel: (020) 7351 0761. www.lafamiglia.co.uk

Giraffe
For global cuisine in a fun environment.
Riverside Level 1, Royal Festival Hall, SE1. Tel: (020) 7928 2004. www.giraffe.net. Open: Mon–Fri 8am–11pm, Sat 9am–11pm, Sun 9am–10.30pm.

Hard Rock Cafe
Come here for a burger and a sighting of Eric Clapton's Lead II Fender.
150 Old Park Lane, W1.
Tel: (020) 7514 1700.
www.hardrock.com.
Open: Sun–Thur 11.30am–12.30am, Fri & Sat 11am–1am.

DID YOU HEAR?

The chimes of St Clement Danes (Strand, WC2) mark the hour. They play the *Oranges and Lemons* nursery rhyme.

Planet Hollywood
Pretend you're in Hollywood and appear on the big screen while you eat.
13 Coventry St, W1.
Tel: (020) 7437 7639.
www.planethollywoodlondon.com
Open: daily 11.30–1am.

Rainforest Café
With plenty of foliage and tropical fish within, this ethically-minded café sponsors rainforest conservation.
20 Shaftesbury Ave, W1.
Tel: (020) 7434 3111.
www.therainforestcafe.co.uk.
Open: Mon–Fri noon–10pm, Sat & Sun 11.30am–10pm.

Smollensky's on the Strand
For an American-style balloons-and-party atmosphere. Booking at weekends is essential. This chain also has a branch at 1 Reuters Plaza, Canary Wharf.

Feeding the birds on the Serpentine at Hyde Park

Peter Pan has been a magnet for children in Kensington Gardens since 1912

105 Strand, WC2. Tel: (020) 7497 2101. www.smollenskys.com. Open: Mon–Wed noon–11pm, Thur–Sat noon–11.30pm, Sun noon–10.30pm.

Tootsies Grill

For burgers and other meaty options in child-sized portions.
*120 Holland Park Ave, W11.
Tel: (020) 7229 8567.
www.tootsiesrestaurants.com.
Open: Mon–Fri 10am–11pm.
Sat & Sun 10am–11.30pm.*

Toy shops

Hamleys in Regent Street is one of the world's biggest toy stores; Disney is nearby on Oxford Street. Model enthusiasts head for Beattie's in Holborn.

V & A Museum of Childhood

A long journey, but worth it to see one of the world's largest displays of toys, including model railways, games, teddy bears, musical toys, dolls and dolls' houses, plus children's costume and nursery furniture.
*Cambridge Heath Rd, E2.
Tel: (020) 8983 5200.
www.vam.ac.uk/moc.
Open: daily 10am–5.45pm.
Free admission.
Tube: Bethnal Green.*

Sport and leisure

Thanks to Britain, sport is one of the common languages of the world. Some games were invented here – golf, tennis, cricket, rugby; others were given rules – football, boxing, track and field athletics, and swimming. Now spectators and participants in every continent yearn to watch or play at Wimbledon, Wembley, Twickenham or Lord's – London's cathedrals of tennis, football, rugby and cricket.

SPECTATOR SPORTS

Athletics
Crystal Palace National Sports Centre
All-star international, as well as local, meets take place here.
Ledrington Rd, SE19.
Tel: (020) 8778 0131. Rail: Crystal Palace.

The Boat Race
Begun in 1829, this annual rowing race takes place in March/April between Oxford and Cambridge universities. The route stretches 7km (4$^1/_3$ miles) from Putney to Mortlake.

Boxing
Wembley Arena
Next to Stadium. Also hosts basketball and ice hockey.
Wembley. Tel: 0870 400 0688.
Tube: Wembley Park.

Cricket
Lord's
The world headquarters of the sport, and venue for Test matches and major finals. Home of Marylebone Cricket Club. (*See p66.*)
St John's Wood, NW8.
Tel: (020) 7616 8500. www.lords.org.
Tube: St John's Wood.

The Brit Oval
Venue for Test matches; home of Surrey County Cricket Club.
Kennington, SE11. Tel: 0871 246 1100.
www.surreycricket.com. Tube: Oval.

Football
Arsenal
The 100-year-old 'Gunners' are among the most famous clubs in the world. Arsenal moved to their plush new Emirates Stadium in 2006.
Emirates Stadium, N5.
Tel: (020) 7619 5000. www.arsenal.com.
Tube: Finsbury Park.

Chelsea
A glamour club that is stacked full with big-money players.
Stamford Bridge, SW6.
Tel: (020) 7915 2900. www.chelseafc.com. Tube: Fulham Broadway.

Tottenham Hotspur
Another club that boasts star performers.
White Hart Lane, N17. Tel: 0844 499 5000. www.tottenhamhotspur.com. Tube: Seven Sisters or White Hart Lane.

Golf
Sunningdale Golf Club
Site of major championships on the European Professional Tour.
Ridgemount Rd, Sunningdale, Berkshire. Tel: (01344) 621 681. www.sunningdale-golfclub.co.uk. Rail: Sunningdale.
Wentworth Golf Club
The club hosts the World Matchplay Championship as well as several European tour events.
Virginia Water, Surrey. Tel: (01344) 842201.
www.wentworthclub.com.
Rail: Virginia Water.

Greyhound racing
London's best-known racetrack, Walthamstow, closed in 2008 but Wimbledon still thrives.
Wimbledon Stadium
Stadium Rd, Plough Lane, SW17. Tel: 0870 840 8905.
Open: Tue, Fri & Sat 6.30pm. Admission charge.
Tube: Wimbledon, Tooting Broadway and by taxi from there.

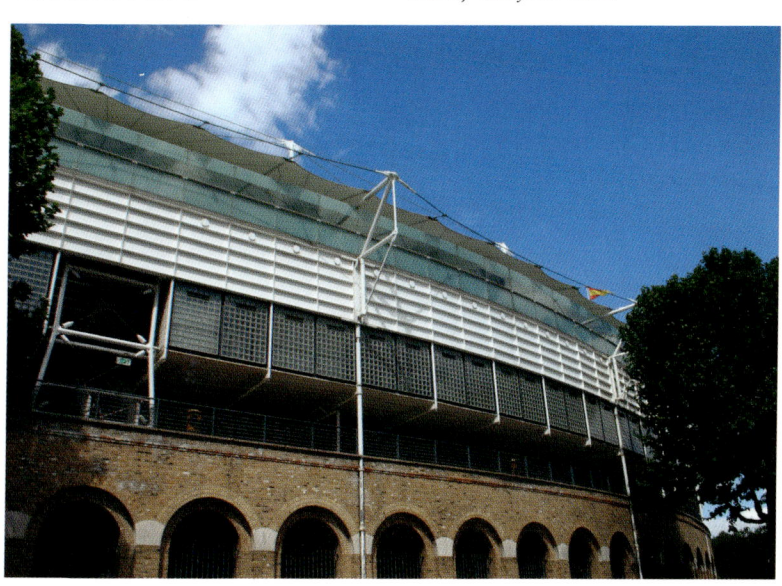

OLYMPIC GAMES 2012
The 2012 Olympic games will take place between 27 July and 12 August 2012. Visit *www.london2012.com* for all the latest Olympic Games Stories and progress.

Lord's: the home of cricket

Horse racing

Ascot Racecourse
With the Queen in attendance, Royal Ascot is the most glamorous race meeting of the year (June), with horses almost taking second place to ladies' hats.
Ascot, Berkshire. Tel: 0870 727 1234. www.ascot.co.uk. Rail: Ascot.

Epsom Racecourse for the Derby (early June).
*Epsom Downs, Surrey.
Tel: (01372) 726311.
www.epsomderby.co.uk.
Rail: Epsom.*

Kempton Park
*Sunbury-on-Thames, Middlesex.
Tel: (01932) 782292.
www.kempton.co.uk.
Rail: Kempton Park.*

Sandown Park
*Esher, Surrey. Tel: (01372) 464348.
www.sandown.co.uk. Rail: Esher.*

TWICKENHAM

Tours of the stadium plus a fascinating World Rugby Museum. *Rugby Football Union, Rugby Rd. Tel: (020) 892 8877. www.rfu.com/microsites/museum.
Open: Tue–Sat 10am–5pm, Sun 11am–5pm. Closed: Mon & Dec 24–26. Admission charge. Stadium Tours: Tue–Sat 10.30am, noon, 1.30pm & 3pm; Sun 1pm & 3pm.
Tube: Hounslow East, then bus 281. Rail: Twickenham, then a 15-minute walk, or take bus 281.*

Windsor
*Windsor, Berkshire. Tel: (01276) 472169.
www.wpec.org.uk.
Rail: Windsor & Eton Riverside.*

London Marathon

Every April the 42km (26-mile) route starts at Blackheath and Greenwich and winds past the *Cutty Sark,* over Tower Bridge, through Docklands, back past

The London Marathon attracts competitors from all over the world

Lord's Cricket Ground is the home of cricket

the Tower of London, the Houses of Parliament, and Buckingham Palace before finishing in The Mall.
For details see:
www.london-marathon.co.uk

Rugby Union
Twickenham
Headquarters of the Rugby Football Union. (*See Tours p160.*)
Twickenham. Tel: (020) 892 8877.
Tube: Hounslow East. Rail: Twickenham.

Tennis
The All England Lawn Tennis Club
Hosts the world's number one tennis tournament, played last week of June, first week of July.
Church Rd, Wimbledon, SW19.
Tel: (020) 8944 1066.
www.wimbledon.org. Tube: Southfields or Wimbledon Park.

Beckenham Tennis Club
Hosts the first tournament of the grass-court tennis season.
Foxgrove Rd, Beckenham, Kent.
Tel: (020) 8650 0266.
www.beckenhamtennisclub.co.uk.
Rail: Beckenham Junction.

Queen's Club
Almost as chic as Wimbledon itself.
Palliser Rd, W14. Tel: (020) 7385 3421.
www.queensclub.co.uk.
Tube: Barons Court.

TOURS
Some of London's most famous sporting venues have museums, and tours which may need to be pre-booked. Lord's, Twickenham and Wimbledon are three of the most important.

LEISURE ACTIVITIES
Dance
Pineapple Dance Studio
Famous as a centre for professional and amateur dancers alike with classes, massage and osteopathy.

7 Langley St, WC1. Tel: (020) 7836 4004.
www.pineapple.uk.com.
Open: daily. Tube: Covent Garden.

Golf

London is ringed by famous but private clubs. However, there are public courses and smaller private clubs that welcome non-members on weekdays. Always telephone ahead and book.

Dulwich and Sydenham Hill

An 18-hole, private and quiet suburban course 8km (5 miles) south of the City.
Grange Lane, College Rd, SE1.
Tel: (020) 8693 3961.
www.dulwichgolf.co.uk.
Rail: Sydenham Hill.

Richmond Park

Two busy 18-hole courses.
Roehampton Gate, Priory Lane, SW15.
Tel: (020) 8876 3205.
www.richmondparkgolfclub.org.uk.
Tube: Richmond.

Horse riding

Kingston Riding Centre

Daily hacks in Richmond Park.
38 Crescent Rd, Kingston-Upon-Thames.
Tel: (020) 8546 6361.
www.kingstonridingcentre.com.
Rail: Norbition.

Ross Nye Riding Stables

A chance to ride in Hyde Park.
8 Bathurst Mews, W2.
Tel: (020) 7262 3791.
Open: daily (except Mon).
Tube: Lancaster Gate.

WIMBLEDON LAWN TENNIS MUSEUM

Every facet of tennis since 1877 is displayed here, with memorabilia and detailed information from the Championships. Films are shown, and visitors can take a guided tour (audio commentary available in eight languages), when they are given a glimpse of the famous Centre Court.
Church Road, SW19. Tel: (020) 8946 6131.
www.wimbledon.org. Open: daily 10.30am–5pm. Admission charge.
Tube: Southfields or Wimbledon Park.

Ice skating

Queens Ice Rink and Bowl

Central London's only major rink. (*See pp152–3 for outdoor rinks.*)
17 Queensway, W2.
Tel: (020) 7229 0172. Open: daily.
Tube: Queensway or Bayswater.

Jogging

Most large London hotels offer jogging trails. London's innumerable parks and squares, canal walks and riverside tow-paths make it ideal for jogging.

PARTICIPATORY SPORTS

There are many private sport and health clubs in London. Sometimes hotels have special membership for their guests. Otherwise, a wide range of public leisure centres cater for squash and swimming, in addition to fitness and weight-training.

Chelsea Sports Centre

Facilities for a dozen sports, plus a solarium and a sports injuries clinic.

Chelsea Manor St, SW3.
Tel: (020) 7352 6985.
www.rbkc.gov.uk/sport. Open: daily. Tube: Sloane Square or South Kensington.

The Gym Covent Garden

A fully equipped gym, plus sauna and sports injuries clinic.
30 The Piazza, Covent Garden, WC2.
Tel: (020) 7836 4835.
www.jubileehallclubs.co.uk. Open: daily. Tube: Covent Garden.

Oasis Sports Centre

Indoor pool and sauna plus sunroof-pool for hot summer days. Also has a ground-level outdoor pool.
32 Endell St, WC2. Tel: (020) 7831 1804.
www.gll.org/centre. Open: daily. Tube: Holborn, Covent Garden or Tottenham Court Rd.

Porchester Centre

Heated pools, also squash, weight-training, sauna and old-fashioned Turkish bath.

Queensway, W2.
Tel: (020) 7792 2919.
www.westminster.gov.uk. Open: daily. Tube: Queensway.

Tennis

All London's indoor courts are in private clubs, so venturing on to public courts demands fine weather!

Lincoln's Inn Fields

Three hard courts in a picturesque big square. You can play where Dickens once walked!
WC2. Tel: (020) 7974 1693.
Open: daily. Tube: Holborn.

Regent's Park

Twelve hard courts on the north side of the park.
York Bridge Inner Circle, NW1.
Tel: (020) 7486 4216. Open: daily. Tube: St John's Wood.

Riding in Hyde Park

Food and drink

'Food, glorious food' cried Oliver Twist in the musical. The children dreamed of hot sausage and mustard, cold jelly and custard. Britain's culinary delights have come a long way since Dickens' day – especially in the last decades. Of course, London has always been known for its ethnic food, but now British dishes have been rediscovered and updated by top chefs. Add in a new generation of home-grown talent like Marco Pierre White and Gordon Ramsay, and gourmets have a real treat in store.

The ★ sign indicates the price of a three-course meal without wine.

★   under £15
★★ £15–30
★★★ over £30

TRADITIONAL BRITISH

M Manze ★
Real pie and mash.
*87 Tower Bridge Rd, SE1.
Tel: (020) 7407 2985.
www.manze.co.uk.
Tube: London Bridge.*

Dorchester Grill Room ★★★
Recently refurbished to provide a stylish but relaxing setting for classic British dishes, with superb roast beef.
*53 Park Lane, W1.
Tel: (020) 7629 8888.
www.dorchesterhotel.com.
Tube: Hyde Park Corner.*

Green's Restaurant Oyster Bar ★★★
Traditional English food including steak and kidney pie and jam roly poly.
*36 Duke St, St James's, SW1. Tel: (020) 7930 4566.
www.greens.org.uk.
Tube: Green Park or Piccadilly Circus.*

Rules ★★★
Unchanged since Dickens's day.
*35 Maiden Lane, WC2.
Tel: (020) 7836 5314.
www.rules.co.uk.
Tube: Covent Garden or Charing Cross.*

Savoy Grill ★★★
Posh but friendly. This will reopen sometime in 2009.
*The Savoy Hotel, Strand, WC2.
Tel: (020) 7592 1600.
Tube: Charing Cross or Embankment.*

Simpsons in the Strand ★★★
Old-fashioned and proud of it! The Grand Divan serves 'traditional' British food.
*100 Strand, WC2.
Tel: (020) 7836 9112. www.simpsonsinthestrand.co.uk.
Tube: Covent Garden, Charing Cross or Embankment.*

MODERN BRITISH

Quality Chop House ★★
A 120-year-old 'café' with big benches. Serves jellied eels and grilled meats with creamy mashed potatoes.
*92–94 Farringdon Rd, EC1. Tel: (020) 7837 5093.
www.qualitychophouse.co.uk. Tube: Farringdon or King's Cross.*

French House Dining Room ★★★
A small room above the French House pub with high ceilings and wooden floors. Serious about traditional British dishes but with a modern twist.
49 Dean St, W1.
Tel: (020) 7437 2477.
www.frenchhousesoho.com.
Tube: Piccadilly Circus.

Oxo Tower Restaurant, Bar and Brasserie ★★★
Modern European cuisine with one of the most spectacular views over London.
Oxo Tower Wharf, Barge House St, SE1.
Tel: (020) 7803 3888.
Tube: Blackfriars.

Roast ★★★
In the railway arches above Borough market, reinventing British classics.
Stoney St, SE1.
Tel: (020) 7940 1300. www.roast-restaurant.com.
Tube: London Bridge.

FISH RESTAURANTS AND OYSTER BARS

Fish Hook ★★
Fish dishes with a twist in this excellent restaurant whose menu features many British fish species.
6–8 Elliott Rd, W4.
Tel: (020) 8742 0766.
www.fishhook.co.uk.
Tube: Turnham Green.

Livebait Restaurant & Bar ★★/★★★
Excellent shellfish and seafood. Noted for its colourful breads and distinctive black-and-white tiles.
21 Wellington St, WC2.
Tel: (020) 7836 7161.
www.livebaitrestaurants.co.uk. Tube: Covent Garden. Other branch:
41 The Cut, SE1.
Tel: (020) 7928 7211.
Tube: Waterloo.
Tel: (020) 7727 4321.

Bentley's ★★★
A visual feast of marble, brass and mahogany décor. Grilled Dover sole, salmon and oysters.
11–15 Swallow St, W1.
Tel: (020) 7734 4756.
www.bentleys.org.
Tube: Piccadilly Circus.

J Sheekey ★★★
Crabs and oysters as well as monkfish and lobster, and modern fish dishes.
28–32 St Martin's Court, WC2. Tel: (020) 7240 2565.
www.j-sheekey.co.uk.
Tube: Leicester Square.

FISH AND CHIPS

Geale's ★
Geale's uses beef dripping on its fish batter for a better flavour.
2 Farmer St, W8.
Tel: (020) 7727 7528.
www.geales.com.
Tube: Notting Hill Gate.

Rock & Sole Plaice ★
This is a bargain in Covent Garden.
47 Endell St, WC2.
Tel: (020) 7836 3785.
Tube: Covent Garden.

Rules is London's oldest restaurant

Sea Shell of Lisson Grove ★★
Big portions, super-fresh fish, traditional puddings.
49–51 Lisson Grove, NW1.
Tel: (020) 7224 9000. www.seashellrestaurant.co.uk.
Tube: Marylebone.

FOREIGN FARE

London offers cuisine from around the world. Most of the following cater for vegetarians, but specialist vegetarian restaurants are also listed.

African
Original Tagines ★★
Absolutely wonderful North African place with a suitably exotic look to it and, of course, great tagines and couscous.
7a Dorset St, W1.
Tel: (020) 7935 1545.
Tube: Baker St.

American
Joe Allen ★★
Popular with showbiz types, journalists, publishers and theatre-goers alike.
13 Exeter St, WC2.
Tel: (020) 7836 0651.
www.joeallen.co.uk.
Tube: Covent Garden.

Belgian
Belgo Centraal ★★
The best place in London for the Belgian speciality mussels and frites. Good daily specials and an extensive range of beers.
50 Earlham St, WC2.
Tel: (020) 7813 2233. www.belgo-restaurants.co.uk.
Tube: Covent Garden.

Belgo Noord ★★
72 Chalk Farm Rd, NW1.
Tel: (020) 7267 0718.

Chinese
There are hundreds of Chinese restaurants in London, many of them in Chinatown itself. Here are just a few.

Imperial China ★★
Fine Cantonese cuisine in a tucked-away setting that really is like being whisked away to China.
25a Lisle St, WC2.
Tel: (020) 7734 3388.
www.imperial-china.co.uk

Mr Kong ★★
Popular for its generous portions and dishes such as venison with ginger, duck and bitter melon.
21 Lisle St, WC2.
Tel: (020) 7437 7341.
Tube: Leicester Square.

Ken Lo's Memories of China ★★★
Modern, upmarket restaurant promoting classic regional dishes ranging from Shantung chicken in hot garlic sauce to crispy shredded beef from Szechuan.
65–69 Ebury St, SW1.
Tel: (020) 7730 7734. www.memories-of-china.co.uk.
Tube: Victoria.

French
Le Mercury ★★
Lightly French menu and very reasonable prices make sure this place is always busy. Try the *entrecôte à l'echalotte*. The wine list is very reasonable too and you have to try hard to run up a bill.
140a Upper St, N1.
Tel: (020) 7354 4088.
www.lemercury.co.uk.
Tube: Angel.

Chez Gérard ★★★
A very Parisian restaurant renowned for its steak-frites and crème caramel.
8 Charlotte St, W1.
Tel: (020) 7636 4975.
www.chezgerard.com.
Tube: Tottenham Court Rd. Branches: 31 Dover St, W1. Tel: (020) 7499

8171. 119 Chancery Lane, WC2. Tel: (020) 7405 0290. The Piazza, Covent Garden Market.
Tel: (020) 7379 0666.
Le Gavroche ★★★
See p169.

Italian
Orso ★★
Showbiz personalities regularly frequent this amiable establishment.
27 Wellington St, WC2.
Tel: (020) 7240 5269.
www.orsorestaurant.com.
Tube: Covent Garden.
Manicomio ★★★
If the weather's fine, the combination of alfresco dining and strongly flavoured Italian food can't be beaten.
85 Duke of York Square, King's Rd, SW3.
Tel: (020) 7730 3366.
www.manicomio.co.uk.
Tube: Sloane Square.

Japanese
Wagamama's ★★
This is a canteen-style noodle bar serving fresh and fast food and healthy drinks.
4 Streatham St, WC1.
Tel: (020) 7323 9223.
www.wagamama.com.
Tube: Tottenham Court Rd. Also at 10a Lexington St, W1.
Tel: (020) 7292 0990.
Matsuri ★★★
Matsuri is Japanese cooking at its absolute best and it has won all kinds of praise and awards for its exquisitely presented and delicately flavoured sushi.
71 High Holborn, WC1.
Tel: (020) 7430 1970.
www.matsuri-restaurant.com.
Tube: Holborn.
Branch: 15 Bury St, SW1.
Tel: (020) 7839 1101.
Tube: Green Park.

The streets of Chinatown are lined with restaurants

Nobu ★★★
Part-owned by Robert de Niro, this minimal-style restaurant is renowned for its imaginative Japanese cuisine.
19 Old Park Lane, W1.
Tel: (020) 7447 4747.
www.noburestaurants.com.
Tube: Hyde Park Corner.

Jewish (Kosher)
Bloom's ★★
Old-fashioned establishment serving traditional Jewish fare.
130 Golders Green Rd, NW11. Tel: (020) 8455 1338. Tube: Golders Green.

Malaysian
Satay House ★★
Authentic Malaysian cuisine. Large portions.
13 Sale Place, W2. Tel: (020) 7723 6763. www.satay-house.co.uk. Tube: Paddington.

Middle East
Al Hamra ★★
Good charcoal-grilled traditional Lebanese dishes.
31–33 Shepherd Market, W1. Tel: (020) 7493 1954. www.alhamrarestaurant. co.uk. Tube: Green Park.

South Asian
A tiny selection from the vast choice of restaurants in this category.
Moti Mahal ★★
With four Moti Mahal restaurants in Delhi, the food is guaranteed to be as authentic as you will find anywhere in central London.
45 Great Queen St, WC2. Tel: (020) 7240 9329. www.motimahal-uk.com. Tube: Covent Garden.
The Red Fort ★★/★★★
This is arguably one of the best Indian restaurants in town.
77 Dean St, W1. Tel: (020) 7437 2525. www.redfort.co.uk. Tube: Leicester Square/ Tottenham Court Rd.
Bombay Brasserie ★★★
Underwent a design refurbishment in 2008. Regional delights include Goan fish curry. One of the first upmarket Indian restaurants in London.
Courtfield Close, Courtfield Rd, SW7. Tel: (020) 7370 4040. www. bombaybrasserielondon. com. Tube: Gloucester Rd.
Chutney Mary ★★★
An inventive cross-over of East and West with many surprising results.
535 King's Rd, SW10. Tel: (020) 7351 3113. www.chutneymary.com. Tube: Fulham Broadway.

Spanish
Navarro's ★★
More than just a tapas bar, Navarro's has very good Spanish wines.
67 Charlotte St, W1. Tel: (020) 7637 7713. www.navarros.co.uk. Tube: Goodge St.

Thai
Nahm ★★★
The stylish Nahm in the ultra-stylish Halkin Hotel raised the stakes for Thai food in London and it's still the best in the city. You can even sign up for a lunchtime cookery class from the Head Chef.
The Halkin, Halkin St, SW1. Tel: (020) 7333 1234. Tube: Hyde Park Corner.

Vegetarian
World Food Café ★★
Delicious vegetarian food inspired by the cuisines of India, Sri Lanka, West Africa, Mexico and Turkey. Set in a pretty painted courtyard, with a bakery and vegan café as neighbours.
14 Neal's Yard, WC2.

STAR SPOTTING

If you want to spot famous faces try: **Blakes**, owned by designer Anouska Hempel (*33 Roland Gardens, SW7. Tel: (020) 7370 6701*); **Langan's Brasserie**, part-owned by Michael Caine (*Stratton Street, W1. Tel: (020) 7491 8822*); **San Lorenzo** (*22 Beauchamp Place, SW3. Tel: (020) 7584 1074*); **The Ivy**, once a favourite with Noël Coward, and now frequented by politicans, literati and thespians (*1 West St, WC2. Tel: (020) 7836 4751*).

*Tel: (020) 7379 0298.
Tube: Covent Garden.*
Rasa ★★★
Excellent South Indian (Keralan) cooking, and the helpful staff will advise you.
*5 Charlotte St, W1.
Tel: (020) 7637 0222.
www.rasarestaurants.com.
Tube: Tottenham Court Rd.
Also at 6 Dering St, W1.
Tel: (020) 7629 1346.
Tube: Oxford Circus.*

FAMOUS PLACES AND CHEFS

Some restaurants are known by their chefs and special dishes, both of which create very high prices. Book ahead.
Fifteen ★★★
Jamie Oliver's restaurant gives disadvantaged youngsters a chance to train as chefs. All profits go to charity.
Westland Place, N1. Tel: 0871 330 1515. www.fifteen.net. Tube: Old Street.
The Capital ★★★
Eric Chavot is a name to reckon with when trying Continental specialities.
*22–24 Basil St, SW3.
Tel: (020) 7589 5171.
www.capitalhotel.co.uk.
Tube: Knightsbridge.*

Gordon Ramsay ★★★
Love him or hate him, he produces the best food in London without question.
*68 Royal Hospital Rd, SW3.
Tel: (020) 7352 4441.
www.gordonramsay.com.
Tube: Sloane Square.*
Le Caprice ★★★
Hidden away behind the Ritz. Difficult to get a table – book in advance.
*Arlington House, Arlington St, SW1.
Tel: (020) 7629 2239.
www.le-caprice.co.uk.
Tube: Green Park.*
Le Gavroche ★★★
The Roux family runs this pricey, Michelin-starred restaurant.
*43 Upper Brook St, W1.
Tel: (020) 7408 0881.
www.le-gavroche.co.uk.
Tube: Marble Arch.*
River Café ★★★
Rose Gray and Ruth Rogers have never let their top Italian standards slip. Relaxed atmosphere, stunning food.
*Thames Wharf, Rainville Rd, W6. Tel: (020) 7386 4200. www.rivercafe.co.uk.
Tube: Hammersmith.*

RESTAURANT BARGAINS

Café in the Crypt ★
The menu includes chilli con carne and cauliflower with peanut sauce.
*St Martin-in-the-Fields Church, Trafalgar Square, WC2. Tel: (020) 7766 1158.
Tube: Charing Cross.*
Diana's Diner ★
Italian and English food in large portions.
*39 Endell St, WC2.
Tel: (020) 7240 0272.
Tube: Covent Garden.*
Thai Metro ★
Dead cheap Thai treat.
*36 Charlotte St, W1.
Tel: (020) 7436 4201.
Tube: Goodge Street.*

More and more pavement cafés are springing up

Afternoon tea

*'Like all man's pleasures, when they first begin,
Tea was a mischief, and almost a sin.'*

So wrote AP Herbert in honour of the 250th anniversary of Twinings, the tea-sellers, who have been in the Strand since 1706. By 1735, brewers were worried that tea might replace ale for breakfast; it did more than that. Nowadays, some 30 million cups of tea are sipped every day in London. It is poured into plastic tumblers, earthenware mugs and fine china cups; it is drunk in cafés and canteens, homes and hospitals.

'Tea' can mean a quick cuppa and a biscuit or it can mean a pot of tea and a cake, perhaps in a museum or department store restaurant. 'Afternoon tea', however, is more like a meal. Traditionally served in tea shops in country towns and villages, or by an indulgent grandmother, the last ten years have seen a revival of the custom of taking afternoon tea in London's grand hotels.

This requires time and an appetite; it starts with dainty sandwiches of cucumber or smoked salmon, continues with scones, strawberry jam and clotted cream thick enough to stand the spoon in, and finishes with a selection of sweet cakes, biscuits and pastries.

The choice of teas ranges from Darjeeling to Earl Grey. Although to the English taste these are best with milk, they can be drunk black or with lemon. Then there are Chinese teas such as Lapsang Souchong, and herbal or fruit teas which have become more popular in recent years.

A leisurely afternoon tea in one of London's luxury hotels is an experience to be savoured, and is served from approximately 3pm onwards.

Scones and jam for tea

Tea has been a mainstay of the British constitution for centuries; Twinings' shop on the Strand has met that demand

Tea in style
All of London's major hotels offer a full afternoon tea (reservations are always advisable). At the following places, it is a particularly special experience. Expect to pay from £12–48. You can also have a more informal tea in department stores and brasseries throughout the city.

Brown's Hotel
Albemarle St, W1.
Dukes Hotel
One of London's hidden gems, where you are treated like aristocracy.
St James's Place, SW1.
The Langham Hilton
Portland Place, W1.
Mandarin Oriental Hyde Park
Views into Hyde Park.
66 Knightsbridge, SW1.
Le Méridien
21 Piccadilly, W1.
The Mountbatten
Monmouth Street, WC2.
The Ritz
Dress up and enjoy the formal service.
150 Piccadilly, W1.

St James's Restaurant
Traditional tea with live piano accompaniment.
Fortnum and Mason, 181 Piccadilly, W1.
The Waldorf Hilton
Occasional tea dances with a small orchestra.
Aldwych, WC2.
Winter Garden, Landmark Hotel
222 Marylebone Rd, NW1.
The Wolseley
Take tea amid grand European elegance.
160 Piccadilly, W1.

London pubs

Ask ten Londoners what makes a good pub and you will get ten different answers – the beer, the landlord, the music, the food, the view. In general, the best pubs are 'locals', part of the community, a meeting place to relax after work and socialise.

In central London these can be hard to find; the visitor must look into side streets and down alleyways, around corners and behind office blocks. Many of them are tucked away but each has its own ambience and clientele. Some are straight out of a Dickens novel, others are full of

Attractive façades, often with etched glass windows, are one way of bringing in the clientele

memorabilia, perhaps from the theatre. Take a quick look inside to see if the atmosphere suits your mood; if not, another pub is always near at hand.

Remember, however, that office workers throng the counters at lunch time between 1pm and 2pm. Aficionados might well recommend drinking 'real ale' (beer brewed the traditional way), but all pubs have a wide range of tipples from European and American beers and lagers to spirits, and from wines to cider (alcoholic) and soft drinks. There is never any pressure to order a traditional foaming pint, though it is worth having a half of bitter just to taste it.

In the last decade, food at reasonable prices has become much more important on the pub scene. Nine out of ten pubs serve food nowadays and, in general, pub food can be better value than the food served in restaurants and fast-food chains.

As for the choice of dishes, pubs first began to diversify when chilli con carne and lasagne were introduced to the traditional British menu of steak-and-kidney pie and ploughman's lunch. During the last few years, the selection of food has grown to include Italian, French and fusion cuisine. Thai food is also now offered in many traditional

A refreshing pint of beer

pubs, and it is commonplace in both central London pubs and those in outlying areas.

The other major change is in opening hours. Since 1988 pubs have been allowed to open when they like between 11am and 11pm, and now they can apply to open later if they wish. In central London, most are open all day, some serving coffee. Few keep to the traditional schedule, closing between 3pm and 5.30pm/6pm. Sunday hours are noon–10.30pm. Children under 14 are not allowed in pubs except those with family rooms (rare in London) or gardens. To save embarrassment, check before the whole family troops into the bar. Please note that there is now a ban on smoking in pubs and all public places.

PUBLIC HOUSES (PUBS)
Central London
Cittie of York
The longest counter in Britain, with a real tavern-like atmosphere.
22 High Holborn, WC1.
Tel: (020) 7242 7670.
Tube: Chancery Lane.

De Hems
A two-storey Dutch pub with plenty of seating on the edge of Soho.
11 Macclesfield St, W1.
Tel: (020) 7437 2494.
Tube: Leicester Square.

French House
Genuine louche Soho atmosphere, and a pub with a wartime and showbiz history.
49 Dean St, W1.
Tel: (020) 7437 2799.
Tube: Leicester Square.

Lamb & Flag
Over 350 years old with memorials to poet John Dryden, who survived a mugging in the pub's alleyway in 1679.
33 Rose St, WC2.
Tel: (020) 7497 9504.
Tube: Covent Garden or Leicester Square.

Museum Tavern
Comfy old-fashioned pub opposite British Museum. Karl Marx supposedly drank here.
49 Great Russell St, WC1.
Tel: (020) 7242 8987.
Tube: Tottenham Court Rd or Holborn.

Prince Regent
Old-fashioned Victorian boozer with good pub grub and wide selection of beers.
71 Marylebone High St, W1.
Tel: (020) 7467 3811.
Tube: Baker Street.

Princess Louise
Victorian mirrors, tiles and furniture.
208 High Holborn, WC1.
Tel: (020) 7405 8816.
Tube: Holborn.

City of London
The Black Friar
Extraordinary Edwardian art nouveau temple; this place has to be seen to be believed.
174 Queen Victoria St, EC4. Tel: (020) 7236 5474. Tube: Blackfriars.

Lamb Tavern
Victorian addition to the Victorian market.
10–12 Leadenhall Market, Gracechurch St, EC3.
Tel: (020) 7626 2454.
Tube: Liverpool St.

Punch Tavern
Have a drink and a laugh at the *Punch* magazine cartoons on the walls.
99 Fleet St, EC4.
Tel: (020) 7353 6658.
Tube: Blackfriars.

Ye Olde Cheshire Cheese
One of London's most atmospheric pubs (even after recent expansion), dating from 1667 – Charles Dickens and Dr Johnson were frequent drinkers here.
Wine Office Court, off Fleet St, EC4.
Tel: (020) 7353 6170.
Tube: Blackfriars.

Ye Old Mitre
A secret even among Londoners, hidden up a narrow alley. The cherry tree trunk inside dates from 1576.
1 Ely Court, off Ely Place, EC1.
Tel: (020) 7405 4751.
Tube: Chancery Lane.

East End
Grapes
Dickens was a visitor to this historic riverside pub, which specialises in seafood.
76 Narrow St, E14.
Tel: (020) 7987 4396.

Tube: Stepney Green.
DLR: Westferry.

WINE BARS AND BRASSERIES

Wines from all over the world can be bought in London. Since the 1970s, wine bars have thrived, offering the chance to sample interesting new wines by the glass. They also have good food, often light meals with good salads. Brasseries and smart cafés, which stay open all day, have also become a feature of central London.

Selected wine bars

Bleeding Heart Tavern
Historic pub but it has a wine list better than most wine bars.
19 Greville St, EC1.
Tel: (020) 7242 2056.
www.bleedingheart.co.uk.
Tube: Farringdon.

Café des Amis
French food and international wines, situated next to Royal Opera House.
11–14 Hanover Place, WC2.
Tel: (020) 7379 3444.
www.cafedesamis.co.uk.
Tube: Covent Garden.

Cork and Bottle
One of the best wine bars. Excellent food and wines, especially from Australia.
44–46 Cranbourn St, WC2.
Tel: (020) 7734 7807.
Tube: Leicester Square.

Ebury Wine Bar
A popular wine bar close to Victoria coach station. Fourteen wines by the glass. Good restaurant.
139 Ebury St, SW1.
Tel: (020) 7730 5447.
www.eburywinebar.co.uk.
Tube: Sloane Square or Victoria.

Hardy's
Good, family-run bar and brasserie tucked away in a quiet corner of Marylebone.
53 Dorset St, W1U.
www.hardysbrasserie.com.
Tel: (020) 7935 5929.
Tube: Baker Street.

Le Metro
A few steps from Harrods, Le Metro offers reasonable prices in an otherwise expensive area.
28 Basil St, SW3.
Tel: (020) 7589 6286.
www.thelevinhotel.co.uk.
Tube: Knightsbridge.

Shampers
Lively haunt of media and publishing types. Excellent buffet and wine list, including forty by the glass.
4 Kingly St, W1.
Tel: (020) 7439 9910.
www.shampers.net.
Tube: Oxford Circus or Piccadilly Circus.

Selected brasseries

Café Boheme
Popular with Soho's in-crowd. Reasonably priced and excellent service.
13–17 Old Compton St, W1.
Tel: (020) 7734 0623.
www.cafeboheme.co.uk.
Tube: Piccadilly Circus.

Café Delancey
Handy for Camden Lock. Food available all day.
3 Delancey St, NW1.
Tel: (020) 7387 1985.
Tube: Camden Town.

The Oriel
Stylish art deco meeting place on Sloane Square; good steaks and salads.
50–51 Sloane Square, SW1.
Tel: (020) 7730 4275.
Tube: Sloane Square.

Hotels and accommodation

A doorman resplendent in top hat, tailcoat and gold braid to greet you? Or a cheerful landlady welcoming you into her own home? London's range of accommodation is vast. By comparison with some cities, a place to lay your head can also be expensive, so it is important to shop around to find the right price in the right area.

Visit London's website (*www.visitlondon.com*) has a searchable list of hotels, motels, guest houses, hostels, self-catering, B&Bs (bed and breakfasts), and caravan and camping options. There are numerous other guides and websites for London accommodation, including Enjoy England (*www.enjoyengland.com*), the official tourist board for England.

Hotel tips

Enjoy England has a 'star' rating system, but this reflects the facilities available rather than the quality of stay you might get. So a 'one star' small hotel may be simple, but will have a warm welcome unmatched by a 'five star' modern but impersonal hotel. Some degree of quality, however, can be indicated by the 'approved', 'commended', 'highly commended' or 'de luxe' additional classification.

Only very small hotels in London are ever completely full, but it is wise to book ahead. Visit London has an Accommodation Service. Visit online at *www.visitlondon.com/accommodation*. Credit card holders can book directly on the Visit London Tourist Accommodation website. London's tourist information centres offer an on-the-spot reservation service (*see Tourist Offices, p187*).

When booking a hotel direct, ask what the price includes. VAT? Service charge? Breakfast?

Hoteliers usually won't bargain over their prices, but if you stay several days (especially at smaller hotels) you may well be able to negotiate some sort of discount.

THE DORCHESTER

A favourite of film stars and socialites, the Dorchester is the grand old lady of London's hotels. Opened in 1931 it overlooks Hyde Park and boasts almost three staff to each bedroom, thus offering its special guests – who pay the price for such exclusive service – the highest standards of personal care and attention.

Even if you are unsure of where you want to stay in London, it is worth booking your first night ahead of time to relieve any stress. After arrival, you can use the tourist board reservation service.

If you feel like a splurge, you can splash out for one special night at a luxury hotel like Claridges or the Ritz ... and use budget accommodation for the rest of your stay.

Compared with the USA, London hotel rooms are small, even cramped! Do not equate size with quality. London's middle-range hotels are the least consistent when it comes to service. Do not expect too much, and hopefully you will be surprised – pleasantly! The British love of a 'cuppa' (tea) ensures that many hotel rooms have a kettle for that quick, free tea or instant coffee. By contrast, minibars are extremely expensive, more suitable for the business account traveller. Telephones are useful in the room but can have shockingly high surcharges for outgoing calls. Save money by using public phone boxes (see p187).

THE CHOICE OF HOTEL
Top of the town

London still boasts some of the world's most famous hotels – Claridges, The Connaught, The Ritz and the refurbished Savoy. Each has antique furniture, rich oil paintings and a reverential hush broken only by high heels clacking on marble floors.

Worldwide

All the major international chains catering for businessmen are represented in London: Hilton, Inter-Continental, Hyatt, Sheraton and Marriott, not forgetting the ubiquitous Forte. The view from the London Hilton on Park Lane is a bonus, as are the locations of the Jumeirah Carlton Tower in Knightsbridge and Le Méridien on Piccadilly.

Plain modern

Groups are often booked into the modern blocks like the Holiday Inn, Scandic Crown, Ibis, Thistle, Mount Charlotte, Novotel and Ramada Inns.

The Ritz, one of London's top hotels

Small is beautiful

Many film stars and personalities book into small but luxurious hotels such as Blakes with its dazzling décor, the Halkin near Buckingham Palace, Dukes and the Stafford, hidden in St James's Place, and the Capital near Harrods.

Within the last 20 years, a new category has opened up: townhouse hotels, offering comfort but no restaurant, usually 20 rooms or fewer – such as L'Hotel, next door to Harrods, and the Abbey Court in Notting Hill Gate.

Bed and breakfast hotels can offer excellent value. Good ones are hard to find, but one is The Aster House in South Kensington.

Most of the simple, family-run B&Bs are so popular and so well used that they inevitably have a worn look, but there are exceptions like the Melita House Hotel in Victoria.

Old-fashioned

A handful of family-run quality hotels survive. Durrant's, off Marylebone High Street, and the Goring, near Victoria Station, are two, but both are in a higher price bracket.

What's new?

Some small hotels have opened up in unexpected but useful areas – the Grange Blooms and the Academy, both in Bloomsbury, and the Delmere in Paddington. All three hotels have their own restaurants.

Traditional

Even in London you can have bed and breakfast in a private home. Rooms are available from as little as £32 a night (a half hour from centre) to £45 or more (in central areas). Call London Bed & Breakfast Agency: *Tel: (020) 7586 2768. www.londonbb.com*

Apartments/self-catering

Just as hotels are classified with 'stars', so 'keys' (1 to 5) are used to rate self-catering accommodation. Apartments are ideal for families, giving flexibility and cutting meal costs. Visit London (*see p176*) has a very good listings ranging from £150 per week for a family room to £1,800 plus per week for a luxury apartment.

Camping/youth hostels

Camping is strictly forbidden in London's parks.

Abbey Wood Caravan Club
Federation Rd, SE2. Tel: (020) 8311 7708. Rail: Abbey Wood.

The Camping and Caravanning Club
Greenfields House, Westwood Way, Coventry CV4 8JH. Tel: 0845 130 7631. www.campingandcaravanningclub.co.uk.
Book ahead for these popular caravan and tent sites. All have hot showers.

Crystal Palace Camping Site
Crystal Palace Parade, SE19. Tel: (020) 8778 7155. Rail: Crystal Palace.

Lee Valley Camping and Caravan Park
Meridian Way, Edmonton, N9. Tel: (020) 8803 6900. Rail: Ponders End.

Hostels

www.yha.org.uk
These are always very busy, so it is advisable to book ahead. YHA membership is required. Contact:

City of London Hostel
36 Carter Lane, EC4. Tel: 0845 371 9012. Fax: (020) 7236 7681.

Earl's Court Hostel
38 Bolton Gardens, SW5. Tel: 0845 371 9114. Fax: (020) 7835 2034.

Generator
A new generation of urban hostel.
Compton Place, 37 Tavistock Place, WC1. Tel: (020) 7388 7666.
www.generatorhostels.com.
Tube: Russell Square.

Holland House
Holland Walk, W8. Tel: 0845 371 9122. Fax: (020) 7376 0667.

Oxford Street Hostel
14 Noel St, W1. Tel: 0845 371 9133. Fax: (020) 7734 1657.

Rotherhithe Hostel
20 Salter Rd, SE1. Tel: 0845 371 9756. Fax: (020) 7237 2919.

St Pancras Hostel
79–81 Euston Rd, NW1.
Tel: 0845 371 9344.
Fax: (020) 7388 6766.

West End Hostel
104–108 Bolsover St, W1.
Tel: 0845 371 9154.
Fax: 0845 371 9155.

Claridges is one of the most fashionable addresses for visitors who can afford it

Practical guide

Arrival

Airports
London has five airports – Heathrow, 24km (15 miles) west of London; Gatwick, 48km (30 miles) south of London; Stansted, 48km (30 miles) northeast; Luton, 56km (35 miles) north; and London City Airport in Docklands.

Entry formalities
No visas are required for holidaymakers from Commonwealth countries (except Bangladesh, Ghana, India, Nigeria, Pakistan, Sri Lanka), European Union countries and some nations like the USA, Japan, Norway and Switzerland.

Transfers
Heathrow: Linked to central London by underground, bus and taxi. The Heathrow Express overground train will take you into London's Paddington station in approximately 20 minutes (*www.heathrowexpress.com*). The underground (40 minutes) is cheapest but may be difficult if taking heavy bags. A taxi is economical for four travellers. The Airbus goes to main hotel areas.
Gatwick: Fast, regular trains connect with Victoria Station in the heart of London. Journey time is 30 minutes (*www.gatwickexpress.com*).
Stansted: Fast, regular trains connect with Liverpool Street Station (*www.stanstedexpress.com*), also with the underground network (Tube) via Tottenham Hale on the Victoria Line. Journey time is 40 minutes.
Luton: The rail line First Capital Connect (Thameslink) has a combined rail and coach link from St Pancras or King's Cross stations via Luton Station (45 minutes).
London City Airport: The Docklands Light Railway links the airport with central London.
Boat, train, coach: Visitors from Europe and Ireland can catch trains and coaches from ports direct to main line stations and coach stations. The new Eurostar terminal at King's Cross St Pancras is now taking its fair share of passengers.

Climate
Unpredictable, despite all the weather forecasts. Rarely extremely hot or extremely cold. Rainwear and a sweater are usually handy. In winter, 10°C (50°F) is a nice day; in summer, 20°C (68°F) has locals in shirtsleeves.

Coach tours
A wide range of full or half-day tours are offered in and around London. The following companies are experienced and use qualified guides:
Evan Evans *Tel: (020) 7950 1777. www.evanevanstours.co.uk;*
Golden Tours *Tel: 0844 880 6981. www.goldentours.co.uk*

If you would like to travel out of town cheaply and independently by coach try

National Express: *Tel: 0871 781 8181.
www.nationalexpress.com*

Crime

London has a reputation for being a fairly safe city. However, do not leave valuables in hotel rooms or visible in vehicles, be vigilant about wallets and bags in crowded areas and on the Tube during rush hours, avoid travelling alone at night and walking through darkened streets or parks. (*See also* Police *p184.*)

Customs regulations

Visitors who have bought goods duty and tax free can bring into Britain: 200 cigarettes or 100 cigarillos or 50 cigars or 250g (9oz) of tobacco; 1 litre (35fl oz) of alcohol over 22 per cent proof or 2 litres (70fl oz) not over 22 per cent proof, plus 2 litres (70fl oz) of still table wine; 60cc (2fl oz) perfume; 250cc (9fl oz) toilet water; and other goods worth £145.

For goods bought duty and tax paid in the EU there is in effect no limit on amounts imported into Britain. However, guide levels exist of: 3200 cigarettes or 400 cigarillos or 200 cigars or 3kg (6.6lbs) of tobacco; 10 litres (17^1/$_2$pt) of alcohol over 22 per cent proof, 20 litres (35pt) not over 22 per cent proof, 90 litres (19^3/$_4$gall) wine (including not more than 60 litres/13gall sparkling) and 110 litres (24gall) beer.

Driving
Car hire

Public transport and taxis are quicker and avoid problems of parking or the congestion charge. For trips out of London, consider taking the train, then renting from the station.

Avis Rent A Car *Tel: 0844 581 0147. www.avis.co.uk*
Europcar *www.europcar.co.uk*
Hertz *www.hertz.com*
Thrifty Car Hire *Tel: (01494) 751500. www.thrifty.co.uk*

Drivers under 24 and over 65 should check with companies about insurance as well as age requirements. British car hire companies only accept full, current driving licences with at least one year's driving experience.

Parking

A single yellow line along the kerb indicates a restriction (times are posted on a nearby lamppost). Double yellow lines mean no parking at all times.

LONDON

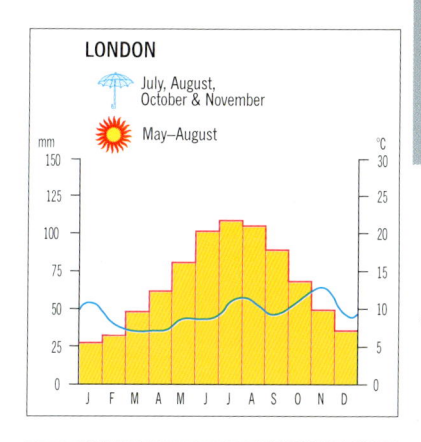

July, August, October & November

May–August

WEATHER CONVERSION CHART

25.4mm = 1 inch
°F = 1.8 × °C + 32

A double red line indicates a priority route for buses along which you may not even stop to set down passengers. Some areas have bays with meters; others use tickets from a nearby machine. Yellow and black uniformed wardens strictly enforce parking regulations; offenders risk being 'clamped' with a metal wheelclamp or towed away. The fines are heavy.

Rules of the road
The British drive on the left. Buy the *Highway Code* for details.

Electricity
British current is 240 volts AC (50Hz). Visitors from the USA and Europe will need a transformer or plug adaptor. Most hotels have special razor sockets which will take both voltages.

Embassies
Australian High Commission
Australia House, The Strand, WC2.
Tel: (020) 7379 4334.
Canadian High Commission
38 Grosvenor Street, W1.
Tel: (020) 7258 6600.
Irish Embassy
17 Grosvenor Place, SW1.
Tel: (020) 7235 2171.
New Zealand High Commission
New Zealand House, 80 Haymarket, SW1. *Tel: (020) 7930 8422.*
United States Embassy
24 Grosvenor Square, W1.
Tel: (020) 7499 9000.

Health
Most European countries have a reciprocal arrangement for free treatment in Britain's National Health Service hospitals. EU nationals with a European Health Insurance Card (EHIC) can consult a National Health Service doctor free of charge and any drugs prescribed can be bought at chemists at prices set by the Health Ministry. No inoculations are required to enter Britain.

Insurance
Visitors from abroad should always take out cover before they leave home. This should encompass belongings, travel arrangements (tickets) and medical cover if there is no reciprocal agreement with Britain.

Internet access
Most hotels now provide wireless and/or high-speed Internet access. London is also full of cybercafés, of varying service and ambience.

Lost property
The London Transport Lost Property Office is at: 200 Baker St, NW1. Open: Mon–Fri 8.30am–4pm. Allow two days for lost items to arrive.
Tel: 0845 330 9882.
Lost on an overground train:
Contact the main line station where train arrived.
Lost in a (black cab) taxi:
Items are handed to nearest police

station and then taken to Baker Street office (see above).
Lost on a coach:
Victoria Coach Station.
Tel: (020) 7730 3466.
Lost in a park:
Contact police for park concerned.
Lost passport:
Contact your embassy or consulate.
Lost credit cards/traveller's cheques:
Follow the instructions given by the issuing company.

In all cases, tell the police in order to validate later insurance claims.

Media

British daily national newspapers range from the 'tabloid', less serious press such as *The Sun,* to '*Berliner*' broadsheets, such as *The Guardian and The Times.* The London *Evening Standard* comes out throughout the day and is a useful guide to what's on in the city. *Time Out* magazine has a weekly round-up of what's on, from music to sport and children's events (*www.timeout.com*).

Money matters

Britain's currency is the pound (sterling) (£). Each pound has 100 pence (p). Coins: £1 and £2 (yellow metal), 50p, 20p, 10p, 5p (silver), and 2p and 1p (copper). Bank notes are £5, £10, £20 and £50.

ATMs, credit cards and traveller's cheques

ATMs are widely available and accept major international networks such as VISA, MasterCard, Cirrus and Plus. Accepted at most shops, restaurants and hotels are VISA and MasterCard; American Express and Diners Club are more upmarket.

Thomas Cook traveller's cheques can be cashed free of commission charge at any Thomas Cook bureau de change (*Tel: 0845 308 9442/9382* to find your nearest branch; *www.thomascook.com*).

Banks

Open usually from 9.30am to 3.30pm (occasionally 4.30pm) and 9.30am to noon on Saturdays. The major banks offer all financial services including a bureau de change. A passport is needed as proof of identity.

VAT

Value Added Tax is a sales tax that can be recouped by visitors from outside the EU for purchases, usually in excess of £50. Before the assistant rings up the purchase at the till, ask for a VAT form. This has to be validated by the customs officer at the departure point. Refunds of the VAT follow later.

National holidays

1 January (or the Monday if 1 January is on a weekend)
Good Friday (before Easter Sunday)
Easter Monday
May Day (first Monday of May)
Spring Bank Holiday (last Monday of May)
Summer Bank Holiday (last Monday in August)

Christmas Day
Boxing Day (26 December, or Monday if Christmas is on a weekend)

Opening hours

Shops: Mon–Sat, 9.30am to 5.30 or 6pm; Sundays noon until 5pm is the norm, although many in the centre of town now stay open until 8 or 9pm on weekdays at least; late-night shopping on Wednesdays in Knightsbridge, and Thursdays on Oxford Street. Small shops stay open later in Covent Garden, while 'convenience stores' stay open late or 24 hours in and around Tube stations, in the West End and in residential suburbs.

Offices: Mon–Fri, 9am to 5.30pm. Lunch is usually 1pm to 2pm when pubs and restaurants in central London are particularly crowded.

Pubs

Most stay open Mon–Sat 11am–11pm, Sun noon–10.30pm. However, some stay open for longer hours.

Pharmacies

A doctor's prescription is required for many drugs.
Bliss Chemist
5–6 Marble Arch, W1.
Tel: (020) 7723 6116. Open: daily 9am–midnight. Tube: Marble Arch.
Boots
44–46 Regent St, W1. Tel: (020) 7734 6126. Open: Mon–Sat 8.30am–8pm, Sun noon–6pm. Tube: Piccadilly Circus.

Also at: 75 Queensway, W2.
Tel: (020) 7229 9266. Open: Mon–Sat 9am–10pm, Sun 2–10pm.
Tube: Bayswater.

Police

999 is the telephone number for real emergencies only. To find the nearest police station, telephone directory enquiries on 118 118.

Post offices

Post offices are generally open weekdays 9am–5.30pm, Sat 9am–12.30pm. The post office near Trafalgar Square on King William IV Street (*Tube: Charing Cross*) is open 8am–8pm, Mon–Sat. Letters to Poste Restante, London, are held here.

Public transport

Avoid the rush hours between 8am and 9.30am, and 5pm and 6.30pm. The one-day Travelcard gives unlimited travel on the Tube, buses, Docklands Light Railway and most overground train services in the London Transport area. The card is valid from 9.30am weekdays, and all day at weekends (*www.tfl.gov.uk*).

Tube

There are no flat fares. The further you go, the more you pay, unless you have a Travelcard or an Oyster Card (*www.tfl.gov.uk/oyster*). Automatic ticket gates 'read' your ticket at both ends of your trip, so always keep it, otherwise you may be liable for an on-the-spot fine.

Bus

Tickets for rides in central London need to be purchased from machines at the bus stop prior to getting on. Nightbuses have an 'N' before the number, and run from about 10.30pm. Most night buses run through Trafalgar Square.

Green Line buses

These single-deck, green-painted buses provide express coach services within a 48km (30-mile) radius of central London. Several run to stately homes and places of interest, with discount vouchers for entry. They depart from: Green Line Coach Terminal, Bulleid Way (off Eccleston Bridge), Victoria, SW1. *Tel: 0844 801 7261. www.greenline.co.uk*

Trains

There is an intricate network of overground lines in London run by different regional companies.
Tickets: You pay by distance, although the Travelcard offers big savings (*www.thetrainline.com*).

River travel

In addition to the trips described on pages 124–9, a Parisian-style boat offers lunch (Sun) and dinner cruises (daily, except Mon), and departs from Temple Pier. For reservations, ring **Bateaux London** (*Tel: (020) 7695 1800. www.bateauxlondon.com*).
The evening cruise has after-dinner live music and dancing, and floodlighting to illuminate riverside buildings.

National Express

A nationwide network of express coaches. Special passes for overseas visitors (*Tel: 0871 781 8181; www.nationalexpress.com*).

Taxis

London's black cabs can be hailed when the orange 'For Hire' sign is lit. The charge on the meter reflects the number of passengers, amount of extra luggage and time of day.
Radio cabs: Some black cabs can be ordered by telephone: *(020) 7222 1234*.
Complaints: Call the Public Carriage Office on *0845 300 7000*, quoting the taxi's licence number.
Mini-cabs: These are not allowed to 'ply for hire' in the street, but must be booked by telephone. Avoid drivers touting for business. This is illegal, and they are probably not insured to carry a paying passenger.

Senior citizens

There are discounts on offer at most museums, galleries and theatres. Senior Citizens Rail Cards (Rail Europe Senior Cards for overseas senior citizens) and National Express Senior Coach Cards offer good reductions. Freedom Pass for London residents permits free travel on London Transport.

Students

An ISIC (International Student Identity Card) is usually recognised. *Time Out* lists many student-orientated activities. Transport discounts are available.

Sustainable tourism

Thomas Cook is a strong advocate of ethical and fairly traded tourism and believes that the travel experience should be as good for the places visited as it is for the people who visit them. That's why we firmly support The Travel Foundation, a charity that develops solutions to help improve and protect holiday destinations, their environment, traditions and culture. To find out what you can do to make a positive difference to the places you travel to and the people who live there, please visit *www.thetravelfoundation.org.uk*

Telephone
Codes
London has a prefix of (020 7) for Inner London, (020 8) for Outer London, and these should be used when calling from one area to the other.

Call boxes
British Telecom (BT) phones accept both small coins (10p, 20p, 50p and £1) as well as phonecards (pre-paid cards available at post offices and newsagents). Some phone boxes can take credit cards too.

Useful numbers
Operator: *100*
International operator: *155*
Directory enquiries: *118 118, 153*
International Direct Dialling is available from all phones, including call boxes. Some useful codes include:

Ireland *00 353*
France *00 33*
Canada *00 1*
USA *00 1*
Australia *00 61*
New Zealand *00 64.*

Thomas Cook traveller's cheques loss or theft: *0800 622101 (freephone)*.
MasterCard loss or theft: *0800 964 767*.
VISA Card loss or theft: *0800 891 725*.

Time
Britain is on Greenwich Mean Time (GMT) in the winter. At the end of March the clocks go forward an hour to British Summer Time until the end of October. Europe is UK + 1 hour, US (West Coast) is UK – 8 hours.

Tipping
Airport/railway porters £1 a bag is welcome. There are now red uniformed Skycaps at Heathrow with a fixed £5 fee per trolley, and at Euston and King's Cross rail stations, with a £2 fixed fee.
Hotels often add a service charge, but porters would expect about £1 per bag.
Restaurants almost always include a service charge. Even if the credit card form is left blank next to tips, do not pay again. If not included, a 10 per cent tip is normal, preferably in cash.
Taxis 10 per cent is normal.
Hairdressers 10 per cent is normal.

Do not feel obliged to tip unless service has been cheerful and efficient.

Tourist offices
Britain and London Visitor Centre:
1 Regent Street, SW1.
Tel: (020) 7808 3801.
Open: Mon–Fri 9.30am–6.30pm,
Sat & Sun 10am–4pm.
Tube: Piccadilly Circus.
Websites
www.visitlondon.com
Official London website.
www.bbc.co.uk/london/travel
Transport and travel information.
www.londontown.com
Comprehensive private travel site.
www.londontourist.org
Unbiased London travel info.
www.londonpass.com
London sightseeing pass information.

Travellers with disabilities
An increasing number of places in London provide facilities for people with disabilities. Helpful services include:
Artsline, a telephone information service advising on disabled access to theatres, galleries and cinemas.
Tel: (020) 7388 2227.
John Grooms Holidays
Organise hotel and self-catering holidays for the disabled. They have arrangements with the Copthorne Tara and Marriott hotels, which have specially adapted rooms.
Tel: (020) 7452 2000.
Restaurant Services
Telephone for advice about accessibility: *(020) 8888 8080.*
Royal National Institute of the Blind (RNIB) *Tel: 0845 766 9999.*

Royal National Institute for the Deaf (RNID) *Tel: 020 7296 8000.*
Guided tours
William Forrester is an award-winning guide and lecturer, and is confined to a wheelchair. He takes groups and individuals (disabled and able-bodied) round London and the UK.
Tel: (01483) 575401.
Book in advance.
Ring Direct Enquiries (*Tel: 01344 360101. www.directenquiries.com*) for information and advice on:
Transport: Mobility Buses with wheelchair access run in London.
Stationlink: wheelchair-accessible buses link mainline railway stations. Wheelchair-accessible airbuses run to Heathrow Airport.

Worship
Every religion is represented somewhere in London. Most of the famous churches are Church of England (Protestant).
Other major religions include:
Catholic: Westminster Cathedral (not the Abbey), Victoria St, SW1.
Tel: (020) 7798 9055.
Jewish: United Synagogue (head office).
Tel: (020) 8343 8989.
Methodist: Methodist Church House.
Tel: (020) 7486 5502.
Muslim: London Central Mosque, 146 Park Rd, NW8.
Tel: (020) 7724 3363.

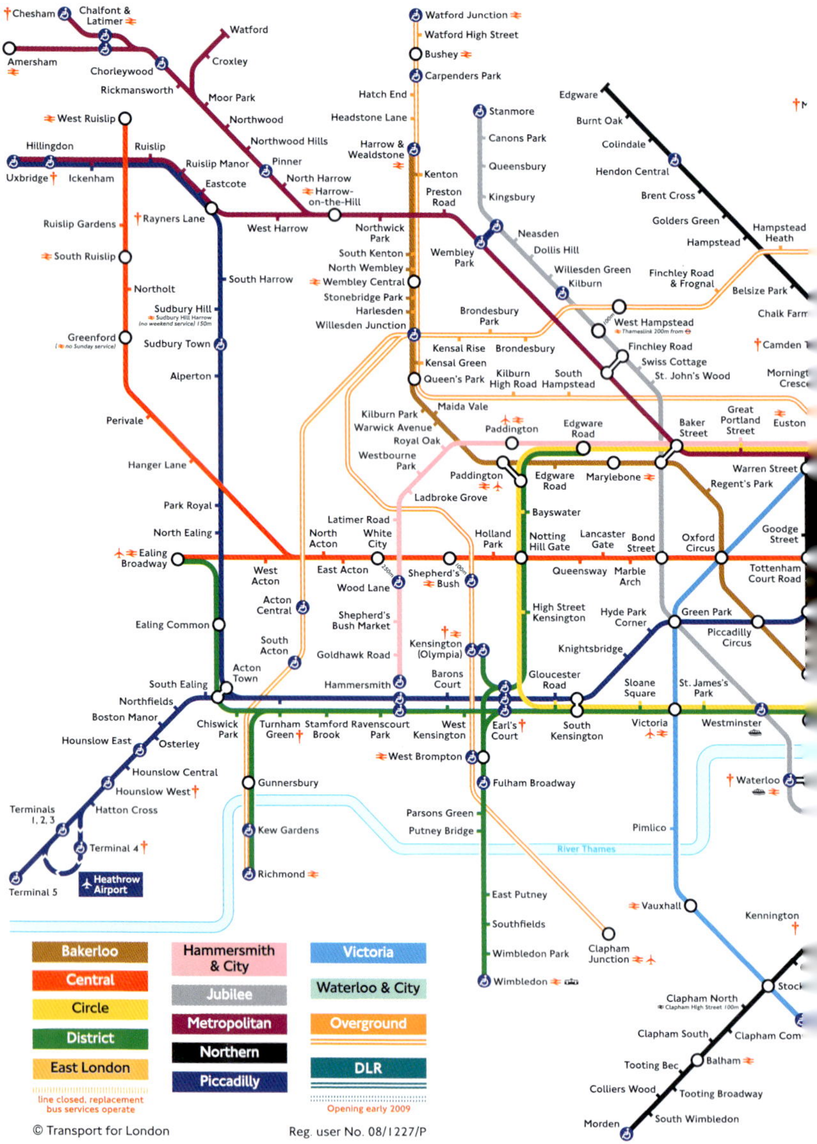

MAYOR OF LONDON

Website
tfl.gov.uk

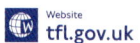

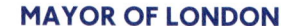

189

Practical guide

Index

A
accommodation 176–9
Admiralty Arch 30
airports and air services 180
Albert Memorial 22, 108
Apsley House 22
areas of London 20–21
Ascot Racecourse 160

B
Bank of England 46
Bank of England Museum 22–3
banks 183
Barbican Centre 23, 45, 148
Bath 132
Battersea Park 119, 152
Big Ben 112
Birdcage Walk 31
Black Friar Pub 48
Blenheim Palace 135
Bloomsbury 21
boat trips 124–9
Borough Market 104, 143
Brighton 132
British Dental Association Museum 62
British Museum 24–5
Buckingham Palace 26–7, 28, 29, 31
bus services 185
bus tours 153–4

C
Cabinet War Rooms 32
Cambridge 132–3
Camden Town 32
camping 178
canal trips 32
Canterbury 133
car hire 181
Carlyle's House 35
Carnaby Street 32
Cartoon Museum 32
Casinos 150
Chancery Lane 69
Changing of the Guard 28
Charles Dickens 52–3
Charing Cross Road 99
Cheapside 46
Chelsea 21, 34–5, 141
Chelsea Physic Garden 34, 120
Cheyne Walk 34–5
children in London 152–7
Chinatown 99
Chiswick 36–7
Chiswick House 36
Christopher Wren 40
churches 35, 36, 38–41, 46, 48, 68
cinema 147
the City 20, 42–9
Clarence House 31
Cleopatra's Needle 33
climate 6, 180, 181
Courtauld Institute 33, 90
Covent Garden 21, 50–51
credit cards 183
crime 181
culture, entertainment and nightlife 12–13, 146–51
currency 183
customs regulations 181
Cutty Sark 130

D
dance 148
Design Museum 103
Dick Whittington 42
Dickens Museum 53
disabilities, travellers with 187
Docklands 20, 54–5
Dorchester Hotel 176
Dover 134
Downing Street 58
Dr Johnson's House 64
driving 181–2
Dulwich 121

E
Eleanor Cross 72
electricity 182
Elgin Marbels 24
Ely Place 49
embassies 182
entry formalities 180
Ethnic London 56–7

F
farms, city 120
Fenton House 62
festivals and events 14–15
Fleet Street 58–9, 68–9
Florence Nightingale Museum 62
food and drink
  eating out 155–7, 164–171, 175
  pubs and wine bars 172–5

Freemasons' Hall 62–3
Freud Museum 63

G
Garden Museum 63
gay and lesbian London 150
Geffrye Museum 59
Gilbert Collection 90
Globe Theatre 104
Golden Hinde 105
Gray's Inn 59–60
Great Court 24–5
Great Fire 70
Green Park 118
Greenwich 130
Guards Museum 27
Guildhall 46, 60
Guy's Hospital 104

H
HMS *Belfast* 103
Ham House 123
Hammersmith 36–7
Hampstead 21, 121–2
Hampton Court Palace 129, 131
Harrods 60–61
Hay's Galleria 105
health 182
Hever Castle 134
Highgate Cemetery 61
history 8–9
Hogarth's House 36
Holland Park 119
Horniman Museum 121
Houses of Parliament 112–13
Hyde Park 118

I
Imperial War Museum 61
Inns of Court 68, 96
Insurance 182
Internet access 182
Isle of Dogs 54–5

J
jazz 148
Jermyn Street 84, 141
Jewish Museum 63
John Nash 26

K
Keats House 64
Kensington 21, 108–9
Kensington Gardens 108, 118
Kensington Palace 64–5, 108

Kenwood House 65
Kew Gardens 122
King's Road 34
Knightsbridge 21, 141

L
Lambeth Palace 65
Law Courts 69, 83
Leeds Castle 134
Legoland Windsor 137
Leicester Square 99
Leighton House Museum 65
Limehouse 54
Lincoln 134
Lincoln's Inn 65–6
Lincoln's Inn Fields 69
Lloyd's of London 44, 47, 66
London Aquarium 153
London Bridge 125
London Dungeon 66, 105
London Eye 23, 124
London, Museum of 74–5
London Oratory 109
London Planetarium 70
London Silver Vaults 70
London Transport Museum 70
London Zoo 70
Lord's 66, 158
lost property 182–3

M
Madame Tussauds 70
Mall 30, 70–71
Mansion House 46, 71
maps
  central London 18–19
  Docklands 54–5
  London environs 20–21
  London Underground 188–9
  Thames 125, 126–7
  see also walks
Marble Arch 72
markets 142–3
Marlborough House 30
Mayfair 21
MCC Museum 66
media 183
Millennium Bridge 124
money 183
Monument 47, 71
monuments, statues and sculptures 22, 32, 71, 72–3, 114–15

Museums
British 24–5
British Dental
Association 62
Cartoon 32
Design 103
Dickens 53
Docklands 76–7
Freud 63
Garden 63
Geffrye 59
Guards 27
Horniman 121, 152
Imperial War 61
Jewish 63
London 74–5
MCC Museum 66
Military 60
National Army 60
National Maritime
125, 130
Natural History 80,
109
Old Operating
Theatre 66–7
Order of St John 66
Royal Airforce 60
Royal Artillery
Museum 60
Rugby 160
Science 88–9
Victoria and Albert
106–7, 109
Westminster Abbey
111

N
National Army Museum
60
National Gallery 78–9
national holidays
183–4
National Maritime
Museum 125, 130
National Portrait
Gallery 80
Natural History Museum
80, 109
Nelson's Column 114
nightclubs 150–151

O
Old Admiralty 115
Old Bailey 48, 81
Old Compton Street
99
Old Royal Naval College
130
Old Royal Observatory
130–31
opening hours 184
opera 50, 148
Order of St John,
Museum of the 66

organised tours 180
Oxford 135

P
Pall Mall 82, 85
parks 116–19
Parliament 112–13
Parliament Square 113
People 6–7, 56–7
Peter Pan 73
pharmacies 184
Piccadilly 85
Piccadilly Circus 82, 98
police 184
pop music 148
post offices 184
public transport 184–5
pubs 172–3, 174, 184

Q
Queen Anne's Gate 31
Queen Boadicea 73
Queen's Chapel 30
Queen Elizabeth II 28
Queen's Gallery 27
Queen's House 131

R
rail services 185
Regent Street 82, 140
Regent's Canal 120
Regent's Park 117, 118–19
Richmond 122–3
Richmond Park 122–3
river travel 124, 185
rock music 148
Rosetta Stone 24
Royal Academy of Arts
82–3
Royal Air Force Museum
60
Royal Albert Hall 108,
148
Royal Botanic Gardens
122
Royal Courts of Justice
69, 83
Royal Exchange 42, 46,
47
Royal Hospital,
Chelsea 34, 83, 120
Royal London 30–31
Royal Mews 27
Royal National Theatre
93
Royal Opera House 50,
148
Rugby Museum 160

S
Saatchi Gallery 90
St Bartholomew-
the-Great 49

St James's 85
St James's Palace 30
St James's Park 30, 119
St James's Street 85
St Leonard's Terrace 34
St Mary-le-Bow 46
St Paul's Cathedral 86–7
sales tax 183
Salisbury 135
Science Museum 88–9
senior citizens 185
Shaftesbury Avenue 98
Shakespeare Trail 136
Shakespeare's Globe
Theatre 104
shopping 138–45
Sir John Soane's
Museum 90
Smithfield 49
Soho 21, 98
Somerset House 90
South Bank Centre 92–3,
148
Southwark Cathedral
105
Speakers' Corner 90–91
Spencer House 67, 85
sport 158–63
Staple Inn 91
State Opening of
Parliament 28–9
Stock Exchange 91
Stonehenge 135–6
Stratford-upon-Avon 136
students 185
sustainable tourism 186
Sutton Hoo Treasure 25

T
Tate Britain;
Tate Modern
Galleries 94–5
taxis 185
tea 170–71
telephones 186
Temple 68, 96
Middle, Inner 96
Temple Bar 96
Temple Church 68
Thames Barrier 96, 125
Thames 124–9
theatre 146–7, 149
Theatre Tickets 146
Thomas Coram
Foundation 67
tipping 186–7
Tomb of the Unknown
Warrior 110
tourist offices 187
tours, organised 180–81
Tower Bridge 97
Tower of London
100–101
ceremonies 103

Trafalgar Square 114
travelling to London
180
Trooping the Colour 28
Twickenham 160

U
Underground system
16, 184, 188–9

V
V & A Museum of
Childhood 157
VAT 183
Victoria and Albert
Museum 106–7,
109
Victoria Tower 113
voltage 182

W
Wallace Collection 67
Wapping 54
West End
20, 98–9, 140, 149
Westminster 21, 112
Westminster
Abbey 110–11
Westminster Hall
112–13
Westminster Abbey
Museum 111
Whitehall 114
Banqueting House
115
Cenotaph 115
Wimbledon Lawn
Tennis Museum
162
Winchester 137
Windsor 137
Wren's House 104–5

Y
youth hostels 179

Acknowledgements

Thomas Cook wishes to thank the photographers, picture libraries and other organisations for the loan of the photographs reproduced in the book, to whom copyright in the photographs belongs.

FLICKR/ZAKGOLLOP 57, 186, SIMPOLOGIST 147, DREAMSTIME 1, 159; FOTOLIA/JEAN YVES YAN LUN 29, BIGSTOCKPHOTO 130, 145a, 151; MUSEUM OF LONDON 74, 75; MUSEUM IN DOCKLANDS 76, 77; OLD OPERATING THEATRE MUSEUM 64; PICTURES COLOUR LIBRARY 7, 39, 58, 61, 89, 144, 157, 161, 169; NEIL SETCHFIELD 13, 25, 32, 33, 43, 44, 45, 51, 53, 56, 59, 62, 63, 67, 71, 74, 79, 82, 85, 90, 93, 95, 101, 102, 111, 113, 117, 139, 142b, 143a, 153, 155, 158, 170, 171, 175, 177; WIKIMEDIA COMMONS/PONTUS ROSEN 65, CHRIS CROOME 83, GREN 91, ARPINGSTONE 96, ANDREW DUNN 107, 133, ATELIER JOLY 130, EDWARD 147, SANDPIPER 149; WORLD PICTURES/PHOTOSHOOT 17, 23, 29, 140, 141, 146, 163, 167.
The remaining pictures are held in the AA PHOTO LIBRARY and were taken by ROGER DAY 41, 87; P BAKER 97; PHILIP ENTICKNAP 136; DEREK FORSS 129; ERIC MEACHER 135; ROBERT MORT 5, 17, 50, 60, 66, 80, 81, 99, 119, 121, 122, 130, 137, 142a, 143b; BARRIE SMITH 11, 123, 151, 154; MARTIN TRELAWNY 27, 169; PETER WILSON 150; TIM WOODCOCK 38, 73.

For CAMBRIDGE PUBLISHING MANAGEMENT LTD:
Project editor: Tom Willsher
Typesetter: Paul Queripel
Proofreader: Frances Darby
Indexer: Marie Lorimer

SEND YOUR THOUGHTS TO BOOKS@THOMASCOOK.COM

We're committed to providing the very best up-to-date information in our travel guides and constantly strive to make them as useful as they can be. You can help us to improve future editions by letting us have your feedback. If you've made a wonderful discovery on your travels that we don't already feature, if you'd like to inform us about recent changes to anything that we do include, or if you simply want to let us know your thoughts about this guidebook and how we can make it even better – we'd love to hear from you.

Send us ideas, discoveries and recommendations today and then look out for your valuable input in the next edition of this title.

Emails to the above address, or letters to Travellers Series Editor, Thomas Cook Publishing, PO Box 227, Coningsby Road, Peterborough PE3 8SB, UK.

Please don't forget to let us know which title your feedback refers to!